DON'T DRESS FOR DINNER

A Comedy

by Marc Camoletti

Adapted by

Robin Hawdon

SAMUEL FRENCH

samuelfrench.co.uk

ISBN 978-0-573-01748-3

www.samuelfrench.co.uk
www.samuelfrench.com

FOR AMATEUR PRODUCTION ENQUIRIES

UNITED KINGDOM AND WORLD
EXCLUDING NORTH AMERICA
plays@samuelfrench.co.uk
020 7255 4302/01

Each title is subject to availability from Samuel French, depending upon country of performance.

THINKING ABOUT PERFORMING A SHOW?

There are thousands of plays and musicals available to perform from Samuel French right now, and applying for a licence is easier and more affordable than you might think

---

From classic plays to brand new musicals, from monologues to epic dramas, there are shows for everyone.

Plays and musicals are protected by copyright law so if you want to perform them, the first thing you'll need is a licence. This simple process helps support the playwright by ensuring they get paid for their work, and means that you'll have the documents you need to stage the show in public.

Not all our shows are available to perform all the time, so it's important to check and apply for a licence before you start rehearsals or commit to doing the show.

LEARN MORE & FIND THOUSANDS OF SHOWS

Browse our full range of plays and musicals and find out more about how to license a show

www.samuelfrench.co.uk/perform

Talk to the friendly experts in our Licensing team for advice on choosing a show, and help with licensing

plays@samuelfrench.co.uk   020 7387 9373

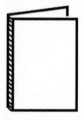

**Other plays by MARC CAMOLETTI
published and licensed by Samuel French**

Boeing-Boeing

Ding Dong

Happy Birthday (Camoletti, Cross adapt.)

FIND PERFECT PLAYS TO PERFORM AT
www.samuelfrench.co.uk/perform

ABOUT THE AUTHOR

Marc Camoletti was a man of many and varied talents, from architect to acclaimed artist to global success as a playwright with over 40 produced plays to his credit. He was also a highly respected theatre director in Paris, responsible for a host of hit productions.

A French citizen, born in Geneva in 1923 with Italian family origins, Marc Camoletti initially trained as an architect. He continued to develop his early talent as an artist which led to five major exhibitions of his paintings in Paris and the provinces, many of his works selling to important private collectors.

Playwriting took over when in 1958 his theatre career got off to a flying start with three plays being presented simultaneously in Paris, the first *La Bonne Anna* running for 1300 performances and going on to play throughout the world.

Marc Camoletti's first great British success was *Boeing Boeing* which, following its West End triumph, also enjoyed a smash hit revival on Broadway. The original 1962 London production ran for seven years at the Apollo and Duchess Theatres, notching up over 2000 performances. The Paramount film version starred Jerry Lewis, Tony Curtis and Thelma Ritter. In 1991, it was listed in the Guinness Book of Records as the most performed French play throughout the world. The Paris revival enjoyed a five year success at the Theatre Michel.

Don't Dress for Dinner, the English language version of the established Paris hit *Pyjamas Pour Six*, also enjoyed a seven year run in the West End opening at the Apollo Theatre and transferring to the Duchess. It was recently revived at the Roundabout Theatre on Broadway. The play has also been performed throughout the United States, as well as in Canada, Australia, New Zealand and South Africa and in different languages throughout the world, always to great acclaim.

His last play, *Sexe et Jalousie*, now titled *Ding Dong* in its English version had a successful Paris production and was the tenth Camoletti play to be shown on television.

In a long theatrical career, Marc Camoletti gained worldwide acclaim through the multitude of productions of his plays in numerous languages in fifty-five countries. In Paris alone 18 of his plays have enjoyed more than 20,000 performances in all.

An Associate of the Societe Nationale des Beaux Arts, Marc Camoletti became a Chevalier de la Legion d'Honeur – one of France's highest honours. He died in 2003.

MUSIC USE NOTE

Licensees are solely responsible for obtaining formal written permission from copyright owners to use copyrighted music in the performance of this play and are strongly cautioned to do so. If no such permission is obtained by the licensee, then the licensee must use only original music that the licensee owns and controls. Licensees are solely responsible and liable for all music clearances and shall indemnify the copyright owners of the play(s) and their licensing agent, Samuel French, against any costs, expenses, losses and liabilities arising from the use of music by licensees. Please contact the appropriate music licensing authority in your territory for the rights to any incidental music.

IMPORTANT BILLING AND CREDIT REQUIREMENTS

If you have obtained performance rights to this title, please refer to your licensing agreement for important billing and credit requirements.

DON'T DRESS FOR DINNER

By Marc Camoletti

Adapted by Robin Hawdon

The Adaptor's name to be no greater than 75% of the size afforded to the author.

DON'T DRESS FOR DINNER

First presented in London by Mark Furness, in association with
Full Circle Productions, at the Apollo Theatre on 20th March
1991 with the following cast of characters:

BERNARD	John Quayle
JACQUELINE	Jane How
ROBERT	Simon Cadell
SUZETTE	Su Pollard
SUZANNE	Briony Glassco
GEORGE	Dougal Lee

Directed by Peter Farago
Designed by Peter Rice

CHARACTERS

BERNARD
JACQUELINE, his wife
ROBERT, his friend
SUZANNE, his mistress
SUZETTE, the cook
GEORGE, her husband

The action takes place in the main living-room of a country house some distance from Paris

Time—the present

ACT I

The main living-room of a country house some distance from Paris. Early evening.

The place is an old farm building converted with style and taste. Upstage is the front door, left is a door off to the kitchen and dining-room. Right is a winding staircase to the upper floor, only the bottom few stairs of which can be seen, downstage left and downstage right are doors to two spare bedrooms. There is a drinks bar, a low sofa, easy chairs, a mirror, and a telephone. Old stone and timber abound. The whole has an atmosphere of affluent rural charm.

When the curtain rises the room is empty.

BERNARD *enters from the kitchen with an ice-bucket and tongs. He is in some haste. He hums to himself as he puts the ice-bucket on the bar, hesitates, then hides it under the bar. He stands back, checking round the room to see if there is anything else needed. He looks at his watch, hurries to the foot of the stairs and calls up.*

BERNARD Hurry up, darling—you're going to be very late.

JACQUELINE *(offstage)* Coming.

He goes to the mirror, smooths his hair and straightens his tie, smiling to himself.

JACQUELINE *comes down the stairs.*

BERNARD *hurriedly turns away from the mirror.*

Darling, I'm so worried about leaving you on your own all weekend.

BERNARD Don't worry, I'll be fine—I've told you.

JACQUELINE You're hopeless at looking after yourself.

BERNARD You've left enough food in the fridge to feed the Foreign Legion.

JACQUELINE It's only frozen canelloni and things.

BERNARD I love canelloni!

JACQUELINE I know, but—

BERNARD Now, do hurry up. You've over an hour's drive and you know how your mother panics if anyone's a minute late.

JACQUELINE Are you sure you can't come with me?

BERNARD She's much happier seeing you on your own. And I can get some work done this weekend. *(Looking at his watch again)* Now get a move on.

JACQUELINE Well, will you bring my case down for me, while I check that you've got everything you need.

BERNARD *(heading for the stairs)* I'm quite capable of defrosting canelloni, you know.

The phone rings. He hesitates on the stairs.

JACQUELINE I'll get it. *(She is nearer and answers the phone before he can do anything)* Go on.

BERNARD *(apprehensively)* Er...right.

BERNARD *vanishes up the stairs.*

JACQUELINE Hallo? ...The what agency? ...Bon Appetit—who are you? ...Tonight? I don't know anything about... Yes, that's me. *(She looks towards the stairs, frowning)* Oh, I see—my husband. Did he, indeed? ...She's leaving now... Suzette. Fine—I'll tell him. Thank you so much. *(She puts the phone down thoughtfully)*

BERNARD *hurries down the stairs with her suitcase.*

BERNARD *(apprehensively)* Who was that?

JACQUELINE The Bon Appetit catering agency.

BERNARD Ah. *(Playing innocent)* Fine.

JACQUELINE Just ringing to say that their girl is on her way.

BERNARD *(heading for the door)* I see.

JACQUELINE Her name is Suzette.

BERNARD *(pausing at the door)* Suzette.

JACQUELINE And everything's arranged for this evening.

BERNARD *(putting down the suitcase)* Perhaps I'd better explain...

JACQUELINE Perhaps you had.

BERNARD I'm not entirely going to totally be absolutely on my own after all.

JACQUELINE Really?

BERNARD No.

JACQUELINE And who is she?

BERNARD *(laughing)* No, no, my sweet—don't get the wrong idea. Robert rang yesterday...

JACQUELINE *(stunned)* Robert?

BERNARD He's just back from Hong Kong. He was at a loose end, and wondered what we were doing this weekend, and—

JACQUELINE Which Robert?

BERNARD *The* Robert. My oldest friend Robert. Our best man Robert.

JACQUELINE Robert is coming here?

BERNARD Yes. Tonight. I didn't mention it because I knew you'd worry about leaving us on our own, and—

JACQUELINE Robert is coming here, and you didn't tell me?

BERNARD He only phoned yesterday, sweetheart, and I didn't want you to start changing plans for our sake. We'll be fine on our own. I'm quite looking forward to it actually.

JACQUELINE He's staying the weekend?

BERNARD Well, tonight and tomorrow. That's why I hired the agency. Bit extravagant, I know, but I wanted to be free over dinner tonight—get a bit pissed, talk over old times, and—

JACQUELINE When's he arriving?

BERNARD *(looking at his watch)* Soon. He's coming down from Paris by train. Going to call me from the station.

JACQUELINE *(dazed)* I see.

BERNARD So you musn't change your plans, darling. You give your mother a nice weekend to keep her going for a while and Robert and I can have a good old-fashioned bachelor time together. It's all organized.

JACQUELINE So it appears.

BERNARD *(looking at his watch again)* You must hurry. She's going to start worrying what's happened to you.

> **BERNARD** *tries to give her the car keys and urge her towards the door. She shows no sign of moving.*

I'll, er... I'll get the car out for you.

> **BERNARD** *gives her a worried look and hurries off out of the front door.*

> **JACQUELINE** *stands in a daze. The phone rings. She answers it.*

JACQUELINE Robert! Robert, where are you—at the station? *(She looks towards the front door to check that* **BERNARD** *has gone)* Robert, he's just told me you were coming! I'm just about to leave for mother's! ...Yes! I've arranged to go to her for the weekend! But I didn't know you were coming, my darling—I've only just found out! Why didn't you call me? ...Well they do have phones in Hong Kong... Oh lord, my angel, I don't know what I can do. How long will you be? It's a two minute taxi ride... Yes, yes... Well leave it with me, I'll try and think of something... I love you too, my precious. Don't worry—I'm not going to miss the chance of a whole weekend with you. Get here as soon as you can. *(She puts the receiver down. She paces frantically. She taps a number on the phone)* Mother? It's me... No, I know I haven't left yet, Mother, but you see I'm—I'm not feeling very well... No, I think it's a touch of flu... Well, I was so looking forward to coming, my dear, but I really don't think I'm up to it. Why don't we make it next weekend? ...Yes, I'm sure I'll be better by then. I'm so sorry to disappoint you, but I promise I'll get over next weekend. 'Bye, Mother. *(She replaces the phone)*

BERNARD *enters.*

BERNARD *(picking up her case)* The car's outside, darling. I'll—

JACQUELINE That was Mother on the phone.

BERNARD Your mother?

JACQUELINE She's got the flu.

BERNARD What?

JACQUELINE She's not well. So I've put it off till next week.

BERNARD *(stunned)* Next week?

JACQUELINE Yes. Isn't that nice? So I can see Robert after all.

BERNARD B-b-but you can't...! You... I...we...

JACQUELINE It's all right, darling, I won't get in the way of your bachelor reminiscences.

BERNARD You must go and look after her! An old lady with the flu like that.

JACQUELINE   Oh, she's got Sophie next door looking after her. She practically ordered me not to come.

BERNARD   But—but...

JACQUELINE   It's fine—I can look after *you* both now. We'll have a lovely time. *(She picks up the phone)* I'll just ring that agency to tell them we'll be one more.

BERNARD   No, no—don't call them!

JACQUELINE   But they'll want to know we're three now.

BERNARD   They know already. I mean, I—I told them we would supply the food, so it doesn't matter how many there are.

JACQUELINE   You were going to give Robert frozen canelloni?

BERNARD   No, I was going to nip into the village and get something special, but—

JACQUELINE   Fine—we can do that now. No problem.

BERNARD   No...yes... Oh dear, I... *(He wanders about distraught)*

JACQUELINE   What's the matter?

BERNARD   Nothing, nothing. I'm delighted. It's—it's just...

JACQUELINE   Is there something you haven't told me?

BERNARD   No, of course not. I've just got to get used to the different plan, that's all.

JACQUELINE   Well, why don't you take my case back upstairs for me, while I get things ready in the kitchen for the girl?

BERNARD   *(dazed)* Yes...right... *(He picks up the suitcase, and goes to the stairs. He stops at the bottom)* Are you sure your mother doesn't need you?

JACQUELINE   Quite sure.

BERNARD   Oh God...

JACQUELINE   What?

BERNARD   Oh good. *(He turns back to the stairs)*

JACQUELINE *(in the kitchen doorway)* By the way, Robert just phoned too. He's on his way.

BERNARD *stumbles on the bottom stair.*

BERNARD *(grinning at her feebly)* Oh, good. *(He turns away)* Oh, God.

BERNARD *goes on up the stairs.*

JACQUELINE *watches him until he is out of sight, then goes to the mirror and preens herself. The doorbell rings. She hurries to the front door and opens it.*

ROBERT *enters with a suitcase, wearing a hat.*

ROBERT Darling!

JACQUELINE Darling!

He takes off his hat and puts down his case.

ROBERT Thank God, you're still here.

JACQUELINE Wild horses wouldn't move me. *(She goes to kiss him)*

ROBERT *(stopping her with his hat between them)* Where's Bernard?

JACQUELINE Upstairs.

ROBERT Where's your mother?

JACQUELINE In bed with flu.

ROBERT Where are you tonight?

JACQUELINE In bed with you.

ROBERT My angel!

They go to kiss again. He stops.

This is crazy, you know.

JACQUELINE He invited you, not me.

ROBERT We'll have to be so careful.

JACQUELINE I'll find a way. Oh, I'm so glad I found out you were coming.

ROBERT You were the only reason I did!

Finally he embraces her, the hat between them. A door closes upstairs.

JACQUELINE He's coming!

He picks up his suitcase again. She puts his slightly battered hat on his head and pushes him back out of the front door. He appears to be just entering.

BERNARD *comes down the stairs.*

ROBERT Hallo!

BERNARD You're here!

JACQUELINE Just.

ROBERT Only just. *(He takes his hat off. He shakes hands)* How are you?

BERNARD Terrific! How was Hong Kong?

ROBERT Terrific! It's er...it's so good to see you both. Thank you for having me...inviting me at such short notice.

BERNARD Oh, we see so little of you.

JACQUELINE Far too little.

ROBERT Well, that's nice. *(He looks round)* Lovely house.

BERNARD Of course, you haven't seen it yet.

ROBERT No.

BERNARD Quite small, but ideal for weekends. Less than two hours from Paris. Jacqueline did it all.

ROBERT *(to her)* So attractive.

BERNARD She has such an eye.

ROBERT A beautiful eye.

BERNARD Have you decided where he's sleeping, darling?

JACQUELINE Um...more or less.

BERNARD *(indicating guest bedroom 1)* You see you could either have that room... *(More enthusiastically indicating bedroom 2)* or this room.

ROBERT Er...

> **ROBERT** *sees* **JACQUELINE** *signalling behind* **BERNARD**'s *back at bedroom 1.*

Well then, that room.

BERNARD *(dismayed)* Oh, are you sure? This room's—

ROBERT *(taking his case)* Yes, that'll be fine.

BERNARD Right. It's the cow-shed!

ROBERT What?

BERNARD This was an old farm building once, you see, before we converted it. This was the main barn. We're upstairs in the loft—where the haymaking goes on—ha, ha. The kitchen's the old dairy, with the dining-room next door in the hen-house—and the other spare bedroom is the piggery.

ROBERT I'm glad I didn't choose that.

JACQUELINE *(opening the door to bedroom 1)* No, this is nicer. Lovely big bed.

ROBERT *(peering in)* Lovely.

> **ROBERT** *carries his case into the room.*

> **JACQUELINE** *provocatively presses against him as he squeezes past her.* **BERNARD** *glances at his watch while* **JACQUELINE** *is not looking, and peers out of the window.*

JACQUELINE *(murmuring)* And don't lock your door tonight.

BERNARD *(turning)* What?

JACQUELINE *(turning to him)* Er...we've got to shop for more tonight.

BERNARD Ah—yes.

JACQUELINE I'd better make a list. What were you planning for dinner?

BERNARD I, er...hadn't really thought.

JACQUELINE You hadn't thought? Oh we must plan a nice meal. Is this Suzette girl a good cook?

BERNARD Cordon bleu, they said. And she serves it all, and washes up afterwards.

JACQUELINE You *were* going to do yourselves proud!

BERNARD Well, you know how Robert likes the little extras in life.

JACQUELINE Yes. Well then, you can come with me.

BERNARD Me? You don't need me.

JACQUELINE Yes, I do.

BERNARD What for?

JACQUELINE To pay the bill.

BERNARD But...

JACQUELINE And carry the bags.

BERNARD Ah.

JACQUELINE And we must hurry—it's getting late.

JACQUELINE *goes into the kitchen.*

BERNARD *(frantically)* Oh, God! Oh, hell!

ROBERT *appears from bedroom 1.*

ROBERT Very nice for a cow-shed, I must say.

BERNARD *(grabbing him urgently)* Quickly, Robert. We've got to think fast here.

977899999

ROBERT Eh?

BERNARD I need your help, old son.

ROBERT What's wrong?

BERNARD *(going to the bar)* Have a drink.

ROBERT *(sitting)* Already?

BERNARD You're going to need it. Usual vodka and tonic?

ROBERT Plenty of tonic, please.

BERNARD Same old Robert. *(Pouring two vodkas)* How long have we known each other, Robert? Fifteen years?

ROBERT Must be.

BERNARD Don't see enough of each other.

ROBERT No.

BERNARD But that doesn't stop us remaining good friends, does it?

ROBERT No, indeed.

BERNARD *(bringing the drinks)* That's why we know we can rely on each other in a crisis.

ROBERT Certainly. What crisis?

BERNARD Hold on to your hat, Robert.

ROBERT My hat?

BERNARD *(sitting beside him on the sofa)* There's something you didn't know about this weekend.

ROBERT What?

BERNARD Jacqueline wasn't supposed to be here.

ROBERT I know, she...no, I didn't know that, no.

BERNARD She was going to go and stay with her mother. Much against her wishes.

ROBERT Her mother's?

BERNARD No, Jacqueline's.

ROBERT Why?

BERNARD She doesn't like leaving me on my own.

ROBERT Ah.

BERNARD But there was something *she* didn't know.

ROBERT What?

BERNARD I wasn't.

ROBERT You weren't what?

BERNARD Going to be on my own. Know why?

ROBERT I was coming.

BERNARD No, not...well yes, but that came later. And that didn't matter, because you'd provide a good alibi anyway.

ROBERT Alibi?

BERNARD Yes.

ROBERT What for?

BERNARD The reason I wasn't going to be on my own.

ROBERT *(puzzled)* Do you think you could elucidate a little?

BERNARD You see, Robert, some time ago I met this girl.

ROBERT Really?

BERNARD Superb. A model. Knock-out!

ROBERT Really?

BERNARD Don't sound so surprised.

ROBERT No, no—it's just...

BERNARD I fell for her—hook, line and sinker.

ROBERT Really?

BERNARD And she fell for me.

ROBERT *Really?*

BERNARD Please don't keep saying really like that!

ROBERT Sorry.

BERNARD The point is, Jacqueline was supposed to be away for the weekend while Suzanne—that's the girl—was here.

ROBERT *(looking round)* Here?

BERNARD It's her birthday. It was all organized, you see, for a nice little celebration. And then the old buzzard got the flu.

ROBERT The girl?

BERNARD Jacqueline's mother!

ROBERT Ah.

BERNARD That's why Jacqueline's still here. She couldn't go. And it's landed me right in it.

ROBERT In what?

BERNARD Use your brains, Robert!

ROBERT Yes, right.

BERNARD She's coming here! She's going to be here any moment.

ROBERT I thought she had the flu.

BERNARD The girl! The girl!

ROBERT Oh, the girl.

BERNARD She's on her way! She was supposed to be on the same train you were on.

JACQUELINE *(the light finally dawning)* Really!

BERNARD Yes, really.

ROBERT I see!

BERNARD You didn't, did you?

ROBERT What?

BERNARD See her.

ROBERT I don't know her.

BERNARD (*making curvaceous gestures*) Oh, you'd have known if you'd seen her.

ROBERT Really?

BERNARD Knock-out! I was supposed to pick her up at the station.

ROBERT You are right in it, aren't you?

BERNARD That's why I need your help.

ROBERT *My* help?

BERNARD Yes.

ROBERT How can I help?

BERNARD I want you to say she's yours.

Pause.

ROBERT My what?

BERNARD Your mistress.

ROBERT My...

BERNARD Yes.

ROBERT No.

BERNARD Robert...

ROBERT No!

BERNARD Robert...

ROBERT *No!*

BERNARD Shhh! Why not?

ROBERT I've already got a... It wouldn't work.

BERNARD It's the only way out.

ROBERT No, no, no. I can't. No, no, definitely not. It couldn't possibly work.

BERNARD Why not?

ROBERT I've never even met her. I don't want to meet her. And even if I had met her I couldn't just turn up with her. I mean what would Jacqueline say?

BERNARD Why should Jacqueline object?

ROBERT Jacqueline 's my... I mean, she's...

BERNARD You're a grown man. You've a perfect right to have a girlfriend.

ROBERT But she knows I haven't got a girlfriend. I've never even mentioned a girlfriend.

BERNARD You have a private life, haven't you?

ROBERT That's my affair.

BERNARD Exactly—and this *is* your affair. Who's to know?

ROBERT I'm to know! Jacqueline's to know. Jacqueline's mother's to know. I can't do it. I won't!

BERNARD You must, Robert. My marriage depends on it.

ROBERT Is that why you invited me here? As an alibi?

BERNARD No, no, not at all.

ROBERT But don't you think I'd have been somewhat in the way?

BERNARD You wouldn't have been sharing the bed with us, old boy.

ROBERT I'm so glad.

BERNARD But when you rang, I thought, well why not? I'd love old Robert to meet her. She's a knock-out!

ROBERT So you said.

BERNARD And it would stop the neighbours talking.

ROBERT Why?

BERNARD They'd think she was with you too.

ROBERT Well she isn't!

The phone rings.

BERNARD *(answering)* Hallo? ...Suzanne—my darling! Where are you—still at the station? ...I know, I'm sorry I'm not there, my angel, but something a bit tricky has turned up. Jacqueline's still here! ...Yes—she's had to cancel her trip to her mother's... No, no, no—don't worry, you don't need to go back. I've worked something out—it's all fixed.

ROBERT No, it isn't.

BERNARD *(gesturing at him)* You remember my friend Robert I was telling you about?

ROBERT No, she doesn't.

BERNARD Yes, the one who's staying here too...

ROBERT No, he isn't.

BERNARD Well he's agreed to pretend you're *his* girlfriend.

ROBERT *(shouting into the phone)* No, he hasn't!

BERNARD *(wrestling him for the phone)* Get off! Get off! *(Into the phone)* It's all right, my angel. Just take a taxi and get here as soon as you can. Then all you have to do is pretend you're with Robert, and Jacqueline won't suspect a thing.

They are practically on the floor, fighting for the phone.

ROBERT No, no!

BERNARD Yes, yes! ...I love you, beautiful. *(He blows kisses down the line. Tearing the phone away from* **ROBERT***'s grasp and replacing it)* There—it's fixed.

ROBERT I refuse! I absolutely, emphatically and categorically refuse!

BERNARD Why? Is it so much to ask my oldest friend to help me out of a jam?

ROBERT It can't work. Think about it.

BERNARD Why not?

ROBERT A whole weekend pretending to be lovers when we've never even met! Jacqueline will see through it in a second!

BERNARD Why should she?

ROBERT For one thing, why haven't we arrived together?

BERNARD She missed the train. Caught the next one.

ROBERT For another, how is it I'll seem to know nothing about her?

BERNARD I'm taking Jacqueline off to the village. Give you time to get to know each other.

ROBERT For another, why is it we don't sleep together?

BERNARD You do.

ROBERT For another... *What?*

BERNARD You'll share the cow-shed.

ROBERT No, no, no...

BERNARD Only temporarily of course. *(Pointing)* Until I arrive and you go into the piggery.

ROBERT I won't do it. Absolutely impossible!

BERNARD But it's so simple.

ROBERT *(apoplectic)* Simple! Simple! It's lunatic! People don't go swanning round the country taking mistresses to friend's houses.

BERNARD Yes, they do.

ROBERT Well *I* don't.

BERNARD What do you do?

ROBERT I visit mistresses in their own... I mean, I don't *have* mistresses. I'm not that sort.

BERNARD But it's the only way out, Robert.

ROBERT No.

BERNARD And I thought you were a true friend.

ROBERT I'm going back to Paris.

BERNARD You can't!

ROBERT I'm leaving now. *(Heading for bedroom 1)* Give Jacqueline my apologies. Tell her I've got an important business meeting I've just remembered I'd forgotten.

ROBERT *vanishes.*

BERNARD *(calling)* Well all right, but I'll still have to tell Jacqueline that Suzanne is your mistresss.

ROBERT *reappears.*

ROBERT Why?

BERNARD What else can I tell her?

ROBERT Well you...

BERNARD It's my only alibi.

ROBERT No, it's not—you can—

BERNARD And Suzanne is on her way. She'll be here any second.

ROBERT Well she—

BERNARD All ready to rush into your arms.

ROBERT Ahhhh! *(He goes into a dance of frustration and hammers his fist on a beam in rage)*

JACQUELINE *comes out of the kitchen and stands watching him for several seconds.*

He becomes aware of her and stops, looking foolish.

Woodworm. You've got woodworm.

JACQUELINE Are you trying to concuss them?

ROBERT Yes...no... I... I'm leaving.

JACQUELINE What?

ROBERT I'm sorry, but I've remembered a very important business meeting. I must go back to Paris at once.

JACQUELINE But you can't!

BERNARD Just what I told him.

ROBERT *(heading back to bedroom 1)* I'm sorry, I must.

JACQUELINE That's ridiculous.

BERNARD Just what I said.

ROBERT It was lovely to see you both again.

JACQUELINE I forbid it!

BERNARD Just what I did.

ROBERT Belt up, you!

BERNARD Tell her the truth, Robert.

ROBERT Just be careful or I might!

BERNARD He's ashamed, you see.

JACQUELINE What about?

BERNARD He won't bring it out into the open.

JACQUELINE What? Bring what out?

BERNARD I've told him to be honest about it.

JACQUELINE *What?*

BERNARD The great affair.

JACQUELINE Affair?

A moan from ROBERT.

BERNARD Yes. Since you're going to be here now, we may as well have it out. I've known for some time, you see.

JACQUELINE You've known?

ROBERT No, no...

BERNARD He told me all about it.

JACQUELINE *(aghast)* What?

ROBERT No, no...

BERNARD He's told *me,* but he's too embarrassed to talk about it in front of you.

JACQUELINE What have you told him?

ROBERT I haven't told anybody anything.

BERNARD Why do you deny it? She's your mistress.

JACQUELINE What?

ROBERT Don't listen to him, Jacqueline.

BERNARD You see? He doesn't want to admit it in front of you.

ROBERT *(shaking his head to* JACQUELINE*)* I didn't say that. I—

BERNARD He's so silly. We're all broad-minded here. We weren't born yesterday, were we?

JACQUELINE *(at a loss)* I—I...

BERNARD There's nothing wrong these days in admitting such a thing. Is there?

JACQUELINE Well...if he's actually told you...

ROBERT I didn't.

BERNARD Yes, he did. And I told him it's perfectly acceptable.

JACQUELINE You did!

BERNARD Yes, I did. *(To* ROBERT*)* So admit it.

JACQUELINE *(hopelessly)* All right. I admit it.

BERNARD *(turning)* You admit it? Admit what?

ROBERT *(hurriedly)* She means she admits she'd find it acceptable that it's acceptable for me to admit it after you've found it acceptable that I'd admitted it to you.

BERNARD Quite.

JACQUELINE Acceptable?

BERNARD Exactly.

JACQUELINE Well, I must say I'm astonished.

ROBERT *(hissing)* No, no.

BERNARD Why?

JACQUELINE That he should have told you.

ROBERT *(hissing)* No, no, not that!

BERNARD Why?

JACQUELINE Well about him and—

BERNARD Suzy?

JACQUELINE What?

BERNARD Suzy. She's called Suzy.

ROBERT I'm going.

> **ROBERT** *goes into bedroom 1.*

JACQUELINE *(perplexed)* Who's called Suzy?

BERNARD She is. *(Calling)* Tell her, Robert.

> **ROBERT** *comes out with his suitcase.*

ROBERT Have to get back to Paris.

JACQUELINE Who's Suzy?

BERNARD *She* is.

ROBERT *(picking up his hat)* Goodbye.

JACQUELINE *Who* is?

BERNARD His mistress!

> **ROBERT** *stops with his back to the audience: He drops the suitcase with a thud.*

JACQUELINE His what?

BERNARD Come on, Robert old man. It's nothing to be ashamed of. Why don't you tell her?

JACQUELINE His what?

BERNARD I mean, why should Jacqueline object?

JACQUELINE *(to* ROBERT*)* Your what?

BERNARD Her name is Suzanne. Suzy for short.

JACQUELINE *(to* ROBERT*)* Is this true?

BERNARD She's a model.

JACQUELINE I don't believe it.

BERNARD Why not?

JACQUELINE He has a mistress?

> BERNARD *nods,* ROBERT *shakes.*

> Called Suzy?

> *Nods and shakes.*

> Who's coming for the weekend?

> *More nods and shakes.*

> That's unbelievable!

ROBERT *(a feeble laugh)* Yes.

BERNARD It's not, it's perfectly natural. You and I spent lots of weekends together before we were married.

JACQUELINE They're getting *married*?

BERNARD Ah, I didn't say that. They're just very friendly. And I said I'd be delighted to see them both for the weekend. And then when he found you were going to be here he got all silly about telling you.

JACQUELINE I bet he did!

ROBERT *has collapsed on to his suitcase in a state of total paralysis.*

BERNARD Why? You understand, don't you?

JACQUELINE I'm beginning to.

BERNARD You don't object, surely?

JACQUELINE What could I possibly object to?

BERNARD You're sounding a bit prudish, my darling.

JACQUELINE Me—prudish? Never! He can bring half the *Folies Bergère* for all I care.

BERNARD *(to* ROBERT*)* There you are!

JACQUELINE So where is she—this Suzy?

BERNARD She'll be here soon. She missed the train they were coming on, and she rang to say she'd caught the next one. That was her on the phone just now.

JACQUELINE Well, well—had it all beautifully organized between you, didn't you?

BERNARD Had we known you weren't going to the old buz—your mother's we'd have consulted you, naturally.

JACQUELINE Naturally. Terrific!

BERNARD *goes to* ROBERT *and leads him gently back to a chair.*

BERNARD There, that wasn't so bad, was it? *(He takes his hat)* You see, Jacqueline's fine about it. So you can forget this stupid appointment in Paris. Just relax here while we go and do the shopping.

ROBERT *(trying to rise)* Can't I come with you?

BERNARD *(pushing him back)* No, no, you must wait for Suzy. She'll be here any moment. He must be here to welcome her, mustn't he, darling?

JACQUELINE *(acidly)* Oh yes, he must be here to welcome her. Well—now that the weekend is going to be a major social event, there are a few more things I'll have to add to the list. *(Hissing at* ROBERT*)* Like rat poison and so on!

She marches into the kitchen.

BERNARD There you are, you see—no problem.

ROBERT *(weakly)* No problem.

BERNARD Though I must say, she didn't take it quite as well as I expected. There's quite a moral side to Jacqueline underneath.

ROBERT *(heading for the drinks)* I need another drink.

BERNARD Help yourself, old man. *(He picks up the suitcase)* You won't be needing this now. *(Taking the case back to bedroom 1)* I can rely on you to do your stuff, can't I, Robert?

BERNARD *goes into the bedroom.*

ROBERT Why not? It's poetic justice, I suppose.

BERNARD *returns.*

BERNARD Eh?

ROBERT Nothing. *(He indicates the vodka bottle)* Get plenty of this stuff while you're out. It's going to be a long night.

BERNARD Attaboy! *(He claps him on the shoulder)*

JACQUELINE *enters with the list and a shopping bag.*

JACQUELINE Right, we'd better hurry. *(She hands the bag to* BERNARD*)* Is lover boy staying or going?

BERNARD Oh, he's staying. He's going to telephone and cancel his appointment while we're at the shops. Aren't you, Robert?

ROBERT *nods dumbly.*

Let's go then.

BERNARD *goes out.*

JACQUELINE *(to* **ROBERT,** *between her teeth)* Bastard! No wonder
you didn't want me to know you were coming!

ROBERT It's not what you think, Jacky, I promise.

JACQUELINE Then what is it?

ROBERT I can't explain right now, but just try to remember
this—she won't be what she seems.

JACQUELINE She's a transvestite?

ROBERT No, no...it's simply that...she's... I'm...he's... *(He is lost
for an explanation)* Oh God!

JACQUELINE He won't help you.

ROBERT Angel, listen—

JACQUELINE Don't angel me. Keep your angels for your Suzy
floozy! *(She goes to the door)* Bastard!

She storms out.

ROBERT Well, that's that. *(He bashes the woodworm again in
a fit of despair, then sobers. He downs his vodka and looks
around and comes to a decision)*

He goes to his room. He returns with the suitcase.

*He gets his hat, puts it on his head and is about to open
the front door when the bell rings. He leaps back like a
startled rabbit. He looks round desperately then tiptoes
towards the kitchen. The bell rings again. He sighs, drops
the suitcase and goes to the front door still wearing the
hat. He opens the door.*

SUZETTE *stands there with a big shopping bag.*

SUZETTE Is this the right house?

ROBERT It is.

SUZETTE Oh, good. *(She steps in)* Good-evening.

ROBERT Good-evening.

SUZETTE I'm Suzy.

He stares at her nonplussed.

Don't look so surprised. Aren't I what you expected?

ROBERT Not at all.

SUZETTE Oh?

ROBERT *(hastily)* I mean, I'm not at all surprised, no. Er...you got here quickly.

SUZETTE I got a lift.

ROBERT Oh—I see.

SUZETTE You going out?

ROBERT Pardon?

SUZETTE You've got your hat on.

ROBERT *(taking it off)* Oh, no. I, er... *(He shakes hands)* How do you do. I'm Robert.

SUZETTE Robert?

ROBERT Bernard's, er...

SUZETTE Oh yes—his friend! You're staying the weekend.

ROBERT That's right.

SUZETTE Yes, I know about that.

ROBERT Yes.

SUZETTE Well, where are, er...?

ROBERT They've gone off to shop for dinner. They left me here to meet you.

SUZETTE Oh good. Then you'd better show me what's what.

ROBERT What's what what?

SUZETTE Where everything is.

ROBERT Oh, that can wait. It's more important we get to know each other first.

SUZETTE *(suspicious)* Get to know each other?

ROBERT Yes.

SUZETTE Why?

ROBERT Well this is going to be one hell of an evening. We must be prepared.

SUZETTE Oh, that's no problem, love. Leave all that to me. I can handle everything.

ROBERT You can?

SUZETTE He told me on the phone what's needed.

ROBERT Yes, but—

SUZETTE Going to be quite a party then, is it?

ROBERT Party isn't the word! Now his wife's here too.

SUZETTE His wife?

ROBERT She changed her mind at the last minute, you see. She was going to be miles away.

SUZETTE Oh, I see. Well, wives usually turn up one way or another. *(She giggles)* Though things would be a lot easier for me if they didn't.

ROBERT I'm sure.

SUZETTE They do get in the way rather.

ROBERT *(bemused)* So it would appear.

SUZETTE But don't worry, I can handle wives all right. I get on very well with them usually.

ROBERT If you don't mind me saying so, you don't seem very worried by all this.

SUZETTE Why should I be? This sort of affair's a doddle for me.

ROBERT You mean it's happened before?

SUZETTE Of course! It happens all the time. I've had to handle far more difficult occasions than this.

ROBERT Really?

SUZETTE Yes—family get-togethers. Parties. Weddings even.

ROBERT Weddings?

SUZETTE Well, I can't just pick and choose to suit myself. I've got to go where the action is, haven't I?

ROBERT I suppose so.

SUZETTE I've got to make a living.

ROBERT Living?

SUZETTE Yes.

ROBERT *(a light dawning)* Oh, I see... You make a proper...er, business of this?

SUZETTE Certainly. I don't do it just for fun.

ROBERT Oh. Bernard didn't tell me that.

SUZETTE What?

ROBERT He didn't say he actually...kept you—on call as it were.

SUZETTE He doesn't. I have lots of clients.

ROBERT What?

SUZETTE He's a new one.

ROBERT Good heavens!

SUZETTE There's a lot of people to cater for in today's society you know. Girls like me are in big demand.

ROBERT They must be.

SUZETTE That's why I work through an agency.

ROBERT Agency! He found you through an agency!

SUZETTE Yes.

ROBERT Huh, model indeed. Poor old Bernard.

SUZETTE What?

ROBERT Nothing. Well I must say, you're very mercenary about it.

SUZETTE Naturally. I don't do it for love, dear!

ROBERT *(coolly)* Evidently.

SUZETTE Right, where do we start?

ROBERT Er...well, I'd better begin by telling you a few things about myself.

SUZETTE Pardon?

ROBERT Who I am, and so on.

SUZETTE I know who you are. The friend.

ROBERT Yes, but...well, you ought to know a bit about me.

SUZETTE Why?

ROBERT This has to be handled carefully. It's a very delicate situation.

SUZETTE Delicate?

ROBERT Of course! His wife's going to be sitting right here at the same table.

SUZETTE Yes?

ROBERT And so is Bernard.

SUZETTE And so are you?

ROBERT Well, yes of course I am, but don't you see—one false move and the balloon could go up.

SUZETTE *(her eye-brows going up)* Oh, I see! She's...

ROBERT Yes!

SUZETTE And he's...

ROBERT Yes!

SUZETTE And you're, um...

ROBERT Pig in the middle.

SUZETTE It's *liaisons dangereuses!*

ROBERT Very *dangereuse.*

SUZETTE Now I understand!

ROBERT You take your time.

SUZETTE Oh, well don't worry about it, dear. I'm quite used to that sort of thing too. I don't need to know any more than I have to.

ROBERT Yes, but that's what I mean. You ought to know the bare minimum—for appearance's sake. Now sit down and listen *very* carefully.

SUZETTE *(bemused)* Right.

ROBERT My name is Robert Dubedat.

SUZETTE *(dutifully repeating after him)* Dubedat.

ROBERT I'm an accountant in Paris.

SUZETTE Paris.

ROBERT I live alone in Montmartre with two cats.

SUZETTE Cats.

ROBERT I'm divorced once, and I'm thirty-five years old.

SUZETTE You don't look thirty-five.

ROBERT Really? How old do I look?

SUZETTE At least forty.

ROBERT Yes, well... I've just had the flu. I was Bernard's best man...

SUZETTE Best man.

ROBERT My hobbies are collecting rare stamps and squash.

SUZETTE Squash.

ROBERT I drive a Citroën, and I had my appendix out six months ago.

SUZETTE Why are you telling me all this?

ROBERT All what?

SUZETTE Your operations and everything.

ROBERT Well, you should know where my scars are at least.

SUZETTE Scars?

ROBERT If we're supposed to be sleeping together.

Pause.

SUZETTE You what?

ROBERT Well obviously! I mean we're going to have to share a room.

SUZETTE What room?

ROBERT *(pointing)* That one.

She goes and peers in.

SUZETTE We're sharing this room together?

ROBERT Yes. It's the cow-shed.

SUZETTE And that bed?

ROBERT Well, only in theory.

SUZETTE Theory?

ROBERT I'll sleep in the chair. And then sneak over to the piggery.

SUZETTE The what?

ROBERT The room over there.

She stares at him perplexed.

There's no need to sound so surprised at all this.

SUZETTE I wasn't planning on staying the night.

ROBERT You... Oh, I see! You were planning on going home after dinner.

SUZETTE Yes. I usually do. Having done the honours.

ROBERT Er...well, it doesn't matter when you do the honours, but you must stay the night.

SUZETTE Why?

ROBERT Jacqueline's expecting you to stay. If you rush off after dinner it will raise all sorts of awkward questions.

SUZETTE How d'you mean?

ROBERT Well, you and I have to keep up the pretence. For the sake of their marriage.

SUZETTE *(light dawning)* Oh, I see! The delicate situation!

ROBERT Yes! *(puzzled)* Bernard told you all this on the telephone.

SUZETTE Yes, but you see I didn't realize you... I didn't know that she... I didn't quite understand what was going on.

ROBERT You didn't?

SUZETTE I was a bit slow on the uptake.

ROBERT You certainly were.

SUZETTE So you want me to pretend to be your, er...

ROBERT Yes.

SUZETTE And then no-one will suspect anything.

ROBERT Exactly.

SUZETTE I get it now.

ROBERT Thank God for that!

SUZETTE How will I know what to say?

ROBERT Ah. Well I've said a bit about myself. You can say what I've said to you, but otherwise don't say a thing. If anyone says anything say nothing except what I say if they say anything to me.

SUZETTE *(after a moment)* I think I'll just keep quiet.

ROBERT Are we all agreed then?

SUZETTE As long as it's only pretence.

ROBERT Well of course—I wouldn't try and take advantage of you.

SUZETTE I'll go along with it then. But I'm afraid it's an extra.

ROBERT Extra?

SUZETTE It's not a usual part of my service—pretending to be someone else's lover.

ROBERT No, but—

SUZETTE Two hundred francs.

ROBERT Two hundred francs!

SUZETTE It's a fair enough price—for what's required.

ROBERT But surely you want to save the situation, just as much as I do? You don't want to see their marriage bust up, do you?

SUZETTE Doesn't really concern me, love.

ROBERT Good God, you stony-hearted—

SUZETTE Here now, steady on. I mean, I've got my reputation to think of.

ROBERT That's the point, isn't it?

SUZETTE And a girl has to make a living.

ROBERT Well, I've heard of exploiting the market, but—

SUZETTE It's not much for a whole charade like that. As well as going to bed with a strange man in a cow-stall.

ROBERT I don't believe this.

SUZETTE Two hundred francs!

ROBERT *(nodding)* Two hundred francs.

SUZETTE *(putting her hand out)* Up front.

Resignedly he takes out his wallet and gives her the money. She hides it down her front.

ROBERT *(watching it disappear)* Very up-front.

SUZETTE Right then—now that's settled, where can I get out of these clothes?

ROBERT I beg your pardon?

SUZETTE Well I'd better start looking the part, hadn't I? I can't do that in this lot. *(She picks up her bag)*

ROBERT What are you going to put on?

SUZETTE I've got a sort of little apron thing in here. I'll just slip into that.

ROBERT Apron?

SUZETTE Very dinky. It covers up to here and down to here. *(She demonstrates a very small apron)*

ROBERT Is that all?

SUZETTE What more do I need? *(She goes towards bedroom 1)*

ROBERT *(heading her off)* No, no, you don't need to go that far! It's not that sort of relationship.

SUZETTE It's a rule of the agency, dear. I must dress for the job.

ROBERT *(wrestling with her)* Not now though, not now.

As he tries to wrestle her away from the bedroom, the front door opens.

JACQUELINE *enters.*

ROBERT *and* **SUZETTE** *are caught in a compromising position.*

JACQUELINE Don't mind us.

ROBERT I was just, er...we were just, er... She's made it.

SUZETTE I made it.

JACQUELINE *(icily)* You looked as though you were both making it.

BERNARD *enters, laden with shopping. He struggles to close the door behind him.*

Well then, introduce us.

ROBERT Er...yes, of course. Jacqueline, this is Suzy. Suzy, this is Jacqueline.

SUZETTE Hallo.

JACQUELINE *(frostily)* Hallo. *(She turns)* And this is Bernard, my husband.

BERNARD *comes downstage.*

Bernard, have you met Suzy, Robert's girlfriend?

BERNARD *is going to shake hands. He stops.*

BERNARD Who?

ROBERT My, er...girlfriend.

BERNARD *freezes, his hand out.*

BERNARD No, no.

SUZETTE Yes—I'm his girlfriend.

BERNARD No! No!

JACQUELINE What?

BERNARD *(caught)* Er—no, no—we haven't met, have we? No. How d'you do. *(He shakes her hand and backs off again past* **JACQUELINE***)*

JACQUELINE So, you've made yourselves at home.

SUZETTE Oh yes—lovely home too. Lovely room.

BERNARD *is making furious signs behind* JACQUELINE's *back.*

JACQUELINE Room?

SUZETTE *(indicating bedroom 1)* Our room.

JACQUELINE *(icily)* Oh, you've shown her the room?

ROBERT *(puzzling at* BERNARD's *signals)* Yes, yes, the room.

SUZETTE *(winking at* JACQUELINE*)* Lovely big bed.

JACQUELINE And the bed.

ROBERT *(still distracted)* Oh yes, the bed. Definitely the bed.

JACQUELINE Well, bully for you!

JACQUELINE *turns.* BERNARD *hastily turns his signals into catching an insect.*

SUZETTE I love big beds. *(She puts her arms around* ROBERT, *playing her part to the hilt)* Especially when I'm with Robert.

JACQUELINE Indeed?

ROBERT *(taking her arms away)* Which isn't that often.

SUZETTE *(hugging him again, still winking at* JACQUELINE*)* We love each other so much.

ROBERT *(struggling)* Well, quite a lot.

BERNARD *is going berserk behind* JACQUELINE's *back.*

SUZETTE And we always will. *(She winks at* JACQUELINE*)* You can count on that, however "delicate the situation".

JACQUELINE How very touching.

ROBERT *(pushing her away)* That's enough!

SUZETTE He's so bashful. He didn't used to be like that. *(She takes a deep breath)* I mean for a divorced accountant living in Montmartre with his stamp collection and two cats it was pretty bold to show me his appendix scar in the back of his

Citröen after playing squash even though he *is* thirty-five years old, wasn't it?

Pause.

JACQUELINE *(bemused)* He's a very fast worker.

ROBERT Do you want to say anything else?

SUZETTE Why? Did I leave something out?

BERNARD *(tired of signalling in vain)* Right, now we've sorted all that out—what about this shopping?

JACQUELINE I'll take it through to the kitchen.

ROBERT *(going to help)* Oh, let me help. *(He grabs one of the bags)*

JACQUELINE *(slapping his hand)* You've got your hands full already.

SUZETTE Well let *me* help.

JACQUELINE *(picking up the bags)* I don't need any help, thank you.

SUZETTE I must do something.

JACQUELINE Why don't you check on his appendix scar?

JACQUELINE *marches off to the kitchen, laden with the bags.*

The door closes with a bang. **ROBERT** *sighs hopelessly.*

BERNARD Right. Who are you?

SUZETTE Me?

BERNARD Yes, you!

ROBERT It's her!

BERNARD Who?

ROBERT You know who.

BERNARD I haven't the faintest idea who.

ROBERT You don't know who?

BERNARD Why do you think I was going bananas there? Trying to keep warm?

ROBERT I didn't know what... You mean that isn't her?

SUZETTE Who?

BERNARD Of course it isn't her.

SUZETTE Who?

ROBERT Then if *that* isn't her—

SUZETTE Who?

ROBERT —who is it?

BERNARD That's what I want to know! Who are you?

SUZETTE I'm his girlfriend.

BERNARD *(to* **ROBERT***)* Is this true?

ROBERT No, no.

SUZETTE Yes!

ROBERT No! That's what I told her to say because I thought she was you-know-who.

SUZETTE Who?

ROBERT But if she isn't, who is?

SUZETTE *Who?*

BERNARD Oh, be quiet, you!

SUZETTE Oo, how rude!

BERNARD *(patiently)* Now, slowly and simply, who are you and what are you doing here?

SUZETTE *(to* **ROBERT***)* Can I tell him?

ROBERT Yes, yes—tell him.

SUZETTE For real?

ROBERT Please.

SUZETTE I'm Suzette—from the agency.

BERNARD The agency?

SUZETTE The cook. From the agency. You should know. You booked me.

BERNARD *(collapsing)* Oh my God!

ROBERT You cooked a book—booked a cook?

BERNARD Yes. For dinner tonight.

ROBERT And that's her?

SUZETTE That's me.

ROBERT *(collapsing beside* **BERNARD***)* Oh my God!

They are practically weeping in each other's arms.

JACQUELINE *enters, and stares.*

JACQUELINE Has she worn you both out already?

They pull themselves together.

By the way, the cook from the agency hasn't arrived yet.

SUZETTE Ah, well, yes—

BERNARD *(leaping up)* Yes! Er...yes, it's true she hasn't, has she?

SUZETTE Yes, you see, I—

BERNARD Was looking out for her, but you haven't seen her, have you?

SUZETTE *(indicating* **ROBERT***)* The point is, he—

BERNARD Hasn't seen a sign of her either—have you?

ROBERT Not a sign, no.

SUZETTE I don't understand—

BERNARD Where she can have got to—no, neither can I.

SUZETTE *(to* **ROBERT***)* Look, will you tell them I'm—

ROBERT Longing to help out if she doesn't get here. I'm sure Jacqueline will appreciate that.

SUZETTE *(exasperated)* The point is—

ROBERT That you're never happier than in the kitchen. She'd be delighted for you to help—wouldn't you, Jacqueline?

JACQUELINE *(bemused)* Overwhelmed.

SUZETTE But what am I supposed to do—

BERNARD When the cook arrives? Well, we'll sort that out when she comes. If she comes. *(Looking at his watch)* It's high time she came.

SUZETTE *(infuriated)* I've had enough of this—

BERNARD Prattle about cooks—I agree. Very boring.

ROBERT Very tedious.

BERNARD So let's have no more talk about it.

ROBERT Topic finished.

BERNARD Banished from the conversation! Understand, Suzette?

SUZETTE *(stunned into submission)* If you say so.

BERNARD *(turning to* **JACQUELINE***)* Good, that's sorted that out.

JACQUELINE *(bemused)* Flogged it to death, I'd say. By the way—Suzette...

SUZETTE Yes?

JACQUELINE The cook's name is Suzette too. How odd.

BERNARD Suzanne.

JACQUELINE What?

BERNARD The cook's name is Suzanne...

SUZETTE I'm Suzette!

BERNARD She's Suzette.

JACQUELINE How do you know the cook's name?

BERNARD Well, I...

JACQUELINE I took the phone call. They told me the cook's name and I told you.

BERNARD They told me yesterday when I cooked the b—booked the cook.

JACQUELINE I see. Funny, I thought they said Suzette.

SUZETTE That's right, Suzette's—

ROBERT gets a hand in front of her mouth.

BERNARD Her name. They're very similar. And both called Suzy for short. You just got them the wrong way round.

JACQUELINE Ah. *(To* ROBERT*)* Well now, have you and your... friend found where everything is—apart from the bed?

ROBERT *(coming to her)* Ah—I wanted to mention about that.

JACQUELINE The bed?

ROBERT You see I'm a very restless sleeper...

JACQUELINE You are... *(Seeing* BERNARD *close by)* You are?

ROBERT So Suzy would quite like to sleep in the other room...

JACQUELINE She would?

ROBERT So I'd get some...she'd get some peace.

JACQUELINE Ah.

ROBERT Would that be all right?

JACQUELINE Quite all right. It's the piggery.

ROBERT She knows.

JACQUELINE Well, where's her case?

ROBERT Er...

SUZETTE *(indicating her bag)* There.

JACQUELINE Is that all you have?

SUZETTE I don't need much—for my job.

JACQUELINE Your job?

SUZETTE Yes, I'm a—

BERNARD *(quickly)* Model! She's a model, isn't she, Robert?

ROBERT *(shrugging)* If you say so.

BERNARD *You* said so.

JACQUELINE *(looking* SUZETTE *up and down)* Well, well, a model? *(Drily)* Yes—you've got the style for it.

BERNARD Well, not only a model. She's an actress too. An actress and a model.

JACQUELINE I see. *(She looks at* ROBERT*)* Well, you seem very suitable for Robert. Come along—I'll show you the piggery.

JACQUELINE *picks up the bag and marches into bedroom 2.*

SUZETTE *puts her hand on her hips and glares at the two men.*

SUZETTE Just what am I supposed—

BERNARD *(hurriedly)* Just play your part, Suzy—there's a good girl.

SUZETTE Do I gather there's another cook coming to take my place?

BERNARD Sort of. You might say we're over-cooked.

SUZETTE Well, it's an extra.

BERNARD What?

SUZETTE Playing actresses.

BERNARD Extra?

ROBERT Two hundred francs.

BERNARD What?

SUZETTE That's right. Two hundred.

JACQUELINE *(calling)* Suzy?

SUZETTE *(holding out her hand)* Well?

BERNARD *(taking out his wallet and giving the notes to her)* Oh all right, all right.

SUZETTE *(stuffing them down her front)* Gawd—I've had some funny jobs in my time...!

SUZETTE *goes into bedroom 2.*

BERNARD Well done, Robert! Brilliant! Einstein couldn't have devised a better cock-up!

ROBERT How was I to know? You didn't tell me you'd cooked a b—booked a cook. Suzy was on her way, you said. Meet her, you said. Find out about her, you said.

BERNARD Well, you didn't, did you?

ROBERT I didn't have time. I was too busy telling her about me.

BERNARD So I noticed—right down to the appendix scar! And a model, I said. A knock-out! Did you look at her?

ROBERT She's not bad.

BERNARD Not bad!

ROBERT Good enough for what you need.

BERNARD *(raising his fist)* Watch it, my friend, watch it!

ROBERT *cowers.*

Anyway, how did you get her to play along with the scheme?

ROBERT Two hundred francs.

BERNARD She's having a good night, isn't she? That's what I gave her.

ROBERT Well, at your age you expect to have to pay for it.

BERNARD *(raising his fist again)* Watch it!

> JACQUELINE *comes back, followed by* SUZETTE.

> **BERNARD** *turns his threat into the search for an imaginary insect on* **ROBERT**'s *jacket.*

Watch it...watch it...there it goes! *(He flicks the insect on to the floor and stamps on it)* Got him! *(He grins innocently at* JACQUELINE*)*

JACQUELINE Still no cook?

BERNARD No.

ROBERT No.

SUZETTE No.

JACQUELINE *(turning to her)* How do you know?

SUZETTE They said so.

JACQUELINE Well—I'd better start the dinner without her.

SUZETTE I'll help.

BERNARD What a good idea!

ROBERT *What* a good idea!

JACQUELINE Thank you, I don't need any help.

BERNARD But she's such a very good cook, darling.

JACQUELINE How do you know?

BERNARD Robert said so.

ROBERT Excellent.

SUZETTE Cordon bleu.

JACQUELINE Really? Well, in that case...

SUZETTE Good. At last I can get back to something I understand!

SUZETTE *goes into the kitchen.*

JACQUELINE *(to* **ROBERT***)* Such class! Congratulations, Robert.

JACQUELINE *follows her off.*

ROBERT Wonderful! I'm now the cook's lover.

BERNARD *(sniggering)* You've hooked a cook.

ROBERT It's not funny, Bernard! This is a disaster.

BERNARD Considering the situation, I think we're managing quite well.

The doorbell rings.

ROBERT
BERNARD } *(together)* So far.

BERNARD *goes to open the front door.*

SUZANNE *enters wearing a chic dress and a beautiful coat. She is carrying a small suitcase.*

SUZANNE *(coolly to* **BERNARD***)* Good-evening.

She hands him the suitcase, walks straight past him, and embraces an astonished **ROBERT***.*

Darling!

BERNARD No, no—not now! Jacqueline's in the kitchen.

SUZANNE *(breaking from* **ROBERT***)* Oh, sorry. *(She holds out her hand)* Good-evening.

ROBERT *stands frozen in a state of stunned shock.*

BERNARD Robert, meet Suzanne.

ROBERT *(hoarsely)* How d'you do.

SUZANNE *(shaking* **ROBERT***'s hand formally)* How d'you do. *(She embraces* **BERNARD***)* Darling!

BERNARD That's better! Happy birthday, angel. *(He takes her coat)*

SUZANNE Careful with my coat.

BERNARD Don't worry. I know how much it cost. What took you so long?

SUZANNE This medieval place. There was only one taxi at the station, and some chauvinist pig barged past me and pinched it.

ROBERT Ah, sorry—that was me. If I'd realized—

SUZANNE Oh, what a shame! We could have shared it.

ROBERT *(with feeling)* That would have saved a great deal of trouble.

BERNARD Never mind—listen carefully, angel. For reasons which I haven't time to explain, we've had to change the plan.

SUZANNE Change the plan?

BERNARD Yes. You're no longer his lover.

SUZANNE I'm not.

BERNARD No.

SUZANNE Why not?

BERNARD He's already got a lover.

SUZANNE Who?

ROBERT The cook.

SUZANNE The cook?

BERNARD She's no longer the cook.

SUZANNE What is she?

BERNARD She's you.

SUZANNE Me?

BERNARD What you were supposed to be.

SUZANNE So who am I?

BERNARD What she was supposed to be.

SUZANNE What's that?

ROBERT The cook.

SUZANNE Ah. *(Outraged)* I'm the cook!

> **JACQUELINE** *enters from the kitchen in time to hear the last sentence.*

JACQUELINE So, you're here at last!

SUZANNE Pardon?

JACQUELINE Do you know what time it is?

SUZANNE *(looking at her watch)* Er...

JACQUELINE We were expecting you nearly an hour ago.

SUZANNE You were?

JACQUELINE Yes. What happened to you?

SUZANNE I missed the, er...

BERNARD Bus!

SUZANNE Bus?

BERNARD Bus.

SUZANNE Bus.

JACQUELINE That's no excuse. The agency should have made sure you were here on time.

SUZANNE Agency?

JACQUELINE Bon Appetit.

SUZANNE Thank you.

JACQUELINE The catering agency! Isn't that who sent you?

BERNARD Of course it was.

SUZANNE Oh...yes, of course it was.

JACQUELINE Well, it's not good enough. I've got guests having to help me in the kitchen!

SUZANNE Er...

BERNARD Don't get angry, darling.

SUZANNE I'm not angry, I just...

BERNARD *gestures frantically.*

Oh.

BERNARD She's here now anyway, darling. And we're very glad to see her. Everything's back to normal.

ROBERT Hah!

BERNARD *(glaring at him)* So let's get on and enjoy the evening, eh?

JACQUELINE *(cooling down)* Very well. Come this way, Miss, er...

BERNARD Suzy.

JACQUELINE Suzy.

JACQUELINE *turns towards the kitchen, then sees* **SUZANNE**'s *coat which* **BERNARD** *is still holding.*

What a beautiful coat. Is that yours?

SUZANNE Er...

BERNARD No! It's Suzy's...er, Suzette's. *(To* **ROBERT***)* Isn't it?

ROBERT Yes, yes, Suzette's.

BERNARD I was just about to hang it up.

JACQUELINE *(looking at the label)* Chanel! It must have cost the earth!

BERNARD *(with feeling)* Twenty thousand francs.

JACQUELINE What?

BERNARD Er... Robert paid twenty thousand francs for it. A birthday present for Suzette. Wasn't it, Robert?

ROBERT Um...yes.

JACQUELINE *(livid)* Well happy birthday, Suzette!

BERNARD Yes, happy birthday, Suzette.

SUZANNE *(aghast)* Yes, happy birthday, Suzette!

> **SUZETTE** *comes out of the kitchen wearing a large apron.*

SUZETTE No, I'm a virgo.

> *They stare at her.*

Er...how do you want the artichokes done?

JACQUELINE Oh, you can leave those now. The cook's here.

SUZETTE The cook?

JACQUELINE Yes, at long last. So you can give her the apron.

SUZETTE But—

BERNARD That's all right, Suzy—just give Suzy here your apron, so she can take over.

SUZANNE Well thank you very much. This *is* going to be a wonderful evening.

JACQUELINE I beg your pardon?

SUZANNE Er...you can leave it to me, madam, to make it a wonderful evening.

JACQUELINE Good. Carry on then. We're having artichokes and sauce velouté, followed by cheese soufflé, then veal à la crème and raspberry pavlova.

SUZANNE We are?

JACQUELINE Yes.

SUZANNE *(looking at* **BERNARD***)* And I'm cooking it?

BERNARD Ahem...yes.

> **SUZANNE** *splutters with laughter.*

JACQUELINE You're cordon bleu, aren't you?

SUZANNE No, I'm vegetarian.

SUZETTE *(sighing)* That's just the sort of menu I love.

BERNARD To eat.

SUZETTE Oh yes, to eat as well—but really I prefer—

BERNARD Look, Suzy, why don't you take your coat and hang it up in your room? *(He puts it round her shoulders)*

SUZETTE *(wide-eyed)* My coat?

BERNARD Yes. The coat Robert gave you.

SUZETTE Robert...?

ROBERT Yes, yes—your birthday present—for being so charming and cooperative. *(Ushering her towards bedroom 2)* Hang it up where it won't get damaged.

SUZETTE Well, thank you very much. I might enjoy tonight after all. *(She does an exaggerated walk to bedroom 2 wearing the coat)*

SUZANNE *(furiously)* I'm glad someone might!

> **SUZANNE** *exits to the kitchen with the apron.* **SUZETTE** *exits to the bedroom.*

JACQUELINE *(looking after* **SUZANNE***)* She seems rather bad-tempered.

BERNARD Well, so would you be, if you'd missed your bus and then been verbally assaulted by your employer.

JACQUELINE I had every right.

BERNARD Not wise to get on the wrong side of the cook, darling.

JACQUELINE Why?

ROBERT She might poison us.

BERNARD *(muttering)* She might too.

JACQUELINE What?

BERNARD Er...he's right too—she might.

JACQUELINE Nonsense. *(Looking after* SUZANNE*)* She's also rather glamorous to be a cook.

BERNARD *(winking at* ROBERT*)* Yes, not bad looking.

JACQUELINE A bit over the top—a touch tarty perhaps.

BERNARD Tarty?

JACQUELINE I'd have thought she could have found easier ways to earn a living.

BERNARD Steady on!

ROBERT The hooker at the cooker—ha, ha.

　　BERNARD *glares at* ROBERT.

JACQUELINE Well that's better than a model with a waddle!

　　JACQUELINE *marches off into the kitchen.*

ROBERT Oh my God, what a mess!

BERNARD Listen, Robert—we've got to find a way to sort this out...

ROBERT That's astute of you.

BERNARD I think we can get through the evening all right without Suzanne blowing her top. As long as she knows the sleeping arrangements are OK.

ROBERT How can they be? She's the cook and the cook's meant to go home after dinner.

BERNARD We'll spin dinner out till it seems too late for her to go home. Then she can sleep in the cow-shed.

ROBERT I'm sleeping in the cow-shed!

BERNARD You'll have to sleep in the piggery.

ROBERT Suzette's sleeping in the piggery!

BERNARD That's all right—Suzette's your mistress. It's natural for you to sleep with her in the piggery.

ROBERT I don't want to sleep with her!

BERNARD Beggars shouldn't be choosers, old boy.

ROBERT And she doesn't want to sleep with me!

BERNARD *(angrily)* Well work on it together!

ROBERT *(pouring himself more vodka)* My *God* what a mess!

BERNARD I don't know what you're complaining about. It's my mess.

ROBERT I'm the one who's in it!

BERNARD Why?

ROBERT Look at it this way. I've ended up sleeping with the real cook in the piggery, instead of sleeping with the false cook in the cow-shed, although I'm actually supposed to be...not supposed to be sleeping anywhere with anyone, and all so that you can leave Jacqueline alone in the hay-loft while you roger the false cook in the cow-shed! It's not so much a mess as a dirty great pile of farmyard manure!

BERNARD Shhh! Keep your voice down or nobody will be rogering anybody.

ROBERT Good—they don't deserve to.

SUZETTE *enters from bedroom 2.*

SUZETTE Now look, will somebody please tell me exactly what I'm supposed to be doing here this evening? Am I a cook, a waitress, a model, an actress, a mistress, a prostitute or a pig-sty attendant?

BERNARD Suzette—I know it seems confusing, but it's really quite simple. Put the original terms of employment out of your head. We just want you to pretend for a few hours that you're Robert's girlfriend, who works as an actress and model. You've come as our guest to have a nice dinner, spend the night—in a bed all to yourself if that's your wish—and enjoy the pleasant company. That's all you have to think about.

SUZETTE Right then.

BERNARD But please remember that you are supposed to be a reasonably sophisticated member of Paris society. Is that too difficult?

SUZETTE It doesn't bother me, love...er, what I mean is, *(she adopts a highly-cultured pose)* that, my dear sir, presents me with absolutely no difficulty whatsoevah—in fact, I shall be deelighted to comply with your eccentric desires—

BERNARD Splendid!

SUZETTE —for the sake of a little extra consideration. Shall we say the mere price of an hors d'oeuvres at the *Ritz?*

ROBERT That's about two hundred francs.

BERNARD *(giving her a note)* God, you strike a hard bargain!

SUZETTE *(stuffing it away)* So kind! Very boring doing that all evening though. Can't I help with the dinner at all?

BERNARD We'd be delighted for you to help—as long as you remember it's in the role of a guest.

SUZETTE Oh, right.

  JACQUELINE enters from the kitchen.

JACQUELINE Well, that's got the dinner started. I need a drink!

BERNARD Good idea! *(He goes to the drinks)* Suzy?

SUZETTE *(playing her part)* Oh, thank you so much—how simply too, too kind. I'd like a double Cointreau frappé with just a teenzy slice of lemon.

JACQUELINE Cointreau? Before dinner?

SUZETTE *(thrown)* Er... *(She recovers)* Oh yes, my dear, it's the chic tipple with the Paris in-crowd—didn't you know?

JACQUELINE *(bemused)* No, I didn't.

SUZETTE You haven't lived!

BERNARD *(quickly)* Right, double Cointreau with lemon. Robert?

ROBERT *(holding out his glass)* Triple vodka—no ice.

   BERNARD *pours the drinks.*

SUZETTE *(caressing **ROBERT** intimately)* Oh, he's so macho, my Robert. Drinks, women, life—he devours them all with such style!

JACQUELINE *(biting)* Oh yes—he's Superman. If it moves, zap it!

ROBERT *(muttering, ducking away from **SUZETTE**'s embraces)* Look, sink your Cointreau and get off to the kitchen, will you?

SUZETTE So suave, my lover. *(To **JACQUELINE**)* Well, my dear, is there really absolutely nothing at all I can do to assist with your little soirée?

JACQUELINE Well, it's very kind of you, but—

BERNARD Perhaps she can help the other Suzy a bit, darling. Two cordon bleus are better than one.

JACQUELINE Well, thank you. If you insist. The other one does seem at a bit of a loss in there...

SUZETTE Oh, my pleasure. *(She takes the drink from **BERNARD**)* Thank you so much—how kind. Well then, I'll just trip into the kitchen and see if I can lend a little hand with the cuisine... *(She does what she imagines to be an elegant walk to the kitchen, and trips over herself, just rescuing her drink)* Oops! *(She grins at **JACQUELINE**)* A little aberration in your carpet there, I think. I must give you the name of my pet carpet mender—he's divine!

   SUZETTE *goes off, sipping her drink.*

JACQUELINE *(after a moment)* Some actress! What sort of a performance is that meant to be?

ROBERT I told her to be on her best behaviour in your house.

JACQUELINE If that's her best behaviour I'd hate to see her when she lets her hair down!

BERNARD *(giving them their drinks)* There's yours, darling. Robert.

ROBERT God, I need this!

JACQUELINE I should think you do. That's an expensive lady you have there.

BERNARD *(muttering)* Not half!

JACQUELINE What?

BERNARD Er...not half as expensive as one would think. Modern mistresses are very self-sufficient, so Robert tells me.

JACQUELINE Not how it looks to me. Twenty thousand francs to keep her in coats is not my idea of self sufficiency.

BERNARD Oh, don't keep going on about the coat! You had a pair of gloves last Christmas.

ROBERT *Two* pairs.

BERNARD What?

ROBERT Nothing.

> **JACQUELINE** *is speechless.*

> **SUZANNE** *enters from the kitchen wearing the apron.*

SUZANNE Well, I seem to be redundant. Suzette has taken over in there.

JACQUELINE Oh, I didn't mean her to...

BERNARD That's all right if she's happy. There'll be plenty for Suzanne to do later. Come and have a drink meanwhile, Suzanne.

SUZANNE That's the best suggestion I've heard so far.

JACQUELINE *(put out)* By all means. Give her a double Cointreau frappé with a teenzy slice of lemon.

SUZANNE A what? No, thank you. I'll have the usual.

JACQUELINE The usual?

SUZANNE *and* BERNARD *freeze.*

SUZANNE Er...my usual vodka Martini with no ice, just a dash of vermouth and an olive if you have one—thank you.

JACQUELINE *(bemused)* Good lord!

SUZANNE Sorry, did I say something wrong?

JACQUELINE *(smiling sweetly)* I don't think that's the chic tipple with the Paris in-crowd any more. Do make yourself at home. I'd better see how my guest is coping with the dinner!

JACQUELINE *storms out to the kitchen.*

BERNARD Oh Christ! Can't you play your part a bit more convincingly, angel?

SUZANNE I like that! I come all the way down here for a nice intimate birthday celebration, and I find myself playing skivvy to a full-sized dinner party and a lot of people I've never met before!

BERNARD You just have to play your part till after dinner, and then we'll be together, I promise you.

SUZANNE How?

BERNARD I'm going to see to it that you have the cow-shed to yourself tonight. We'll get Jacqueline totty—she sleeps like a log when she's had a few—then I'll slip down and see you.

SUZANNE And, er...is Robert going to be in there too?

BERNARD Certainly not. I'm kicking him into the other room.

SUZANNE Poor Robert.

BERNARD Poor Robert! He was the cause of all this chaos in the first place!

ROBERT I damn well wasn't. You're the one whose mother-in-law got flu!

BERNARD You're the one who mistook the cook for my girlfriend!

ROBERT You're the one who cooked the b—booked the cook in the first place!

SUZANNE *(coming between them)* Boys! Boys! Calm down. It's too late to fight about it now. We'll manage somehow. *(Stroking* **BERNARD***)* Just as long as you sort it out by tonight.

BERNARD *(going weak)* Ohhhh! Leave it to me, angel. I'll sort it out.

SUZANNE *(seductively)* Good.

BERNARD We'll all get what we want in the end.

ROBERT *(standing beside them)* That's very good to know.

BERNARD
SUZANNE } *(together)* Mmmmm! *(They embrace)*

JACQUELINE walks in.

ROBERT smacks BERNARD across the head and BERNARD's vodka goes flying, soaking his shirt-front.

ROBERT Got it! Got it! Another one! *(He stamps on the floor)*

There is a stunned silence.

(to **JACQUELINE***)* You ought to be doing something about all these insects, Jacqueline. You're infested.

BERNARD *(turning and seeing her)* Ah—I'll, er... I'll go and change my shirt. *(He grins feebly)* I wanted to clean up for dinner anyway.

BERNARD goes upstairs.

SUZANNE I'll, er...just get back to the kitchen, and get on with my job.

SUZANNE *goes into the kitchen.*

JACQUELINE *stares at* ROBERT.

ROBERT I'll, er... *(He drains his glass)* I'll just have another drink. *(He heads for the drinks)*

JACQUELINE Haven't you had enough? You're going to be pissed as a newt before we sit down to dinner at this rate.

ROBERT I need to be.

JACQUELINE I don't know what *you've* got to worry about. You should be very happy. Got your harem all round you.

ROBERT Jacqueline, darling, believe me it's not how it looks.

JACQUELINE That's good, because it looks pretty sordid.

ROBERT Well if you must know, I think it was pretty sordid of us anyway—trying to get together under your own roof with Bernard here.

JACQUELINE Don't start moralizing to me. You don't object when we're in Paris.

ROBERT *(coming close)* That's different. Please, Jackie, this is a very delicate situation...

SUZETTE *enters, wearing another apron and carrying her glass of Cointreau.*

They break apart.

SUZETTE *(playing her part)* Oh, don't mind me. I'm used to these delicate situations. Have them all the time in Paris. I just came in to ask if you desire us to lay the table? I presume we are dining through there in what I'm given to understand was the hen-house?

JACQUELINE Yes, thank you—that's very kind. You'll find everything in the oak sideboard.

SUZETTE *(pouring herself more Cointreau)* Leave it all to me. I'm a dab hand at chucking china round chicken-coops.

SUZETTE *exits, swigging her drink.*

JACQUELINE Well all I can say is you have the most eccentric taste in women!

ROBERT I promise you, she is not my woman.

JACQUELINE What is she then—your pet parrot?

ROBERT She's...

JACQUELINE Well?

ROBERT As a matter of fact she's...

JACQUELINE What?

ROBERT My niece.

JACQUELINE Your *what?*

ROBERT Shhh! It's true.

JACQUELINE What kind of a fool do you take me for?

ROBERT It's true! Think about it, my darling. She didn't want to share my room, did she?

JACQUELINE Because she knows you're a restless sleeper. I know that, and it certainly isn't because you're part of the family!

ROBERT In her case it is. If she'd been my mistress, would I have brought her here to meet you?

JACQUELINE Bernard told you I was going to be at my mother's.

ROBERT But when I rang from the station and you said you'd find a way of staying, I'd have put her on the first train back to Paris.

JACQUELINE That's true.

ROBERT You see?

JACQUELINE Then why is she all over you with her macho-lover act?

ROBERT She's playing a part.

JACQUELINE Playing a part?

ROBERT She is an actress.

JACQUELINE Why?

ROBERT To throw Bernard off the scent. You see, when he invited me down, he said I could bring a girlfriend if I wanted. And I suddenly thought that would be a very good idea—so that he wouldn't suspect what was going on between you and me.

JACQUELINE *(after a moment)* Oh, I see! She's actually...?

ROBERT Yes!

JACQUELINE She isn't really...?

ROBERT No!

JACQUELINE Well why didn't you *tell* me?

ROBERT I never got a chance to. Bernard was always around.

JACQUELINE *(flinging her arms around him)* Oh, my angel, I didn't realize! What a clever idea!

ROBERT Yes, I thought it was quite clever.

JACQUELINE Oh, I'm so glad!

They go into a deep embrace.

SUZETTE *walks in again.*

They break.

SUZETTE Well, it looks to me as if the delicate situation is getting more indelicate by the minute!

JACQUELINE It's all right. Don't worry, Suzette, I know all about you.

SUZETTE You do?

JACQUELINE He's told me everything!

SUZETTE *Everything?*

ROBERT Yes, everything.

SUZETTE You mean, she knows that I'm really...

ROBERT My niece!

SUZETTE *(after a moment)* Your niece?

ROBERT *(nodding)* My niece.

She takes a deep breath.

SUZETTE For the usual?

ROBERT The usual.

SUZETTE Right—I'm your niece. I just came in to get another little drink, and to say, Uncle, that dinner will be ready in about ten minutes. That is, subject to any further family revelations, earthquakes, or pornographic developments.

JACQUELINE Wonderful! *(She kisses* ROBERT*)* I'm so happy. I must just go up and change for dinner.

ROBERT Do I need to change?

JACQUELINE No, my angel. Those clothes are fine. In any case you won't be wearing them much longer.

JACQUELINE kisses him again, and trips happily up the stairs.

ROBERT preens himself at his ingenuity. SUZETTE holds out her hand. He sighs, and reluctantly gives her another couple of banknotes.

SUZETTE You're playing a dangerous game, Uncle.

ROBERT You don't have to tell me. But understand, you're only my niece for her.

SUZETTE What am I for them?

ROBERT My mistress.

SUZETTE What am I for you?

ROBERT The cook.

SUZETTE I should get an Oscar for this!

ROBERT You've done well enough as it is! And lay off that Cointreau! It's far too strong to take before dinner.

SUZETTE *(vamping)* The stronger they come, the better I like 'em!

> **SUZANNE** *enters from the kitchen, still wearing her apron, carrying a bowl of sauce and a wooden spoon.*

SUZANNE I'm not sure if I'm doing this sauce salute right.

SUZETTE Velouté.

SUZANNE Whatever it's called.

SUZETTE *(in her most affected tone)* Well, don't look at me, my dear, you're the cook.

SUZANNE *(indignantly)* I certainly am not the cook!

SUZETTE Then what are you doing here?

SUZANNE That's a very good question!

ROBERT Shhh! Look, you've both got to play your parts for a little while longer.

SUZANNE A little while! It looks as if I've got to play it all over dinner! I'm even supposed to wait on you at table!

SUZETTE Well yes, that does require a certain *savoir faire.* Don't you think you're up to it, my dear?

SUZANNE *(threatening her with a spoonful of sauce)* I'm up to it all right! I'll—

ROBERT *(hastily intervening)* Girls, girls—you can't ruin it all now. You've *got* to keep it up!

SUZANNE Why?

SUZETTE Yes, why?

ROBERT Because you're getting paid for it, and you're getting laid for it... I mean, you've made your bed and you've got to lay on it... I mean... Oh God! *(He takes another drink)*

SUZANNE Isn't he sweet?

SUZETTE Adorable.

SUZANNE Why couldn't I fall for a man like that?

SUZETTE Keep your hands off—he's mine! *(She vamps* **ROBERT**, *stroking his head)* Aren't you, lover? *(She pinches his bottom)*

ROBERT Get off!

SUZETTE *beams and heads for the Cointreau.*

BERNARD *hurries down the stairs, newly dressed.*

BERNARD Now then, girls, is everything set? Do you all understand your roles?

SUZETTE Oh, yes.

SUZANNE I'm not playing mine much longer.

BERNARD Darling! Angel! Just a little longer, and then everything will be all right, I promise. *(He turns to* **SUZETTE***)* Now, Suzette, there's just one more little thing...

SUZETTE Don't tell me. I'm your long-lost daughter who's really a prima ballerina in disguise and I've got to spend the night in the piggery with three of your nephews, a herd of pigs and a prize bull.

BERNARD Er...not quite. I want you to let Robert here share your room over there, so that Suzanne here can have that one over there.

SUZETTE *(taking a long, hard look at the room, then at* **ROBERT***)* That one is *really* going to come expensive!

BERNARD Two hundred.

SUZETTE Four hundred.

BERNARD Three hundred.

SUZETTE Two hundred.

BERNARD Four hundred.

SUZETTE Done!

> *He hands over the notes. She puts them away in the usual place.*

ROBERT Good God!

> **BERNARD** *hesitates, suspecting something wasn't quite right somewhere. He dismisses it.*

BERNARD Now then, Suzette, have you got anything to wear for dinner?

SUZETTE What's wrong with this?

BERNARD It's hardly suitable for the chic girlfriend of a sophisticated man like Robert.

SUZETTE Well, all I've got is my other outfit in there.

BERNARD It must be better than that. Let's see it on.

SUZETTE I don't think it's quite the thing...

BERNARD *(irritably)* Just let us see it, and we'll tell you if it's all right.

SUZETTE *(shrugging)* If you say so.

> **SUZETTE** *goes off to bedroom 2.*

BERNARD *(taking SUZANNE in his arms)* There you are, you see? That's sorted out the bedrooms.

SUZANNE It's not sorting out the bedrooms that worries me.

BERNARD What is it?

SUZANNE Sorting out the dinner.

BERNARD Don't worry about a thing, my angel. All you have to do is...

JACQUELINE comes down the stairs, dressed in a low-cut evening outfit.

ROBERT again cracks BERNARD smartly across the head, and stamps on the imaginary insect. BERNARD leaps. The contents of SUZANNE's bowl end up down BERNARD's shirt-front. Long pause. SUZANNE tries ineffectively to scrape his shirt clean with her wooden spoon.

(eventually) I'll just go and put on another shirt.

BERNARD passes JACQUELINE with a feeble smile and goes out.

JACQUELINE What in heaven's name is going on in here?

ROBERT It's all my fault. I have this thing about people getting stung.

JACQUELINE Stung?

ROBERT Yes. It's been happening rather a lot tonight.

SUZANNE Yes, well... I'll go and make some more sauce polluté.

JACQUELINE Velouté!

SUZANNE Bless you.

SUZANNE goes off to the kitchen.

ROBERT *(gazing at JACQUELINE)* You look stunning!

JACQUELINE *(coming close)* Like it, angel?

ROBERT *(gazing down her front)* Both of it. Beautiful!

Just as they are about to kiss, she smacks him hard on the cheek.

JACQUELINE Pig!

ROBERT *(stunned)* What...? What's the matter?

JACQUELINE *(producing two pieces of paper)* This is the matter! A receipt and a note which I've found. *(Reading from one)* "One coat. Twenty thousand francs to the house of Chanel."

ROBERT Er...so?

JACQUELINE And this is the note. *(Reading from the other)* "My angel. Thank you for the gorgeous, gorgeous coat, you gorgeous, gorgeous man. Suzy."

ROBERT How sweet.

JACQUELINE You know what these mean?

ROBERT They mean I'm heavily overdrawn, I imagine.

JACQUELINE Wrong. I found them in Bernard's jacket pocket when I hung it up to dry.

ROBERT Ah.

JACQUELINE Which means that *you* didn't buy that coat for your niece, as I suspected all along. It means that Bernard did. And you know what that means?

ROBERT It means I'm not as overdrawn as I thought I was.

JACQUELINE It means that she is Bernard's mistress. Which *you* knew all along. *(Advancing on him)* It means you've been covering up for that swine all evening.

ROBERT Now, Jackie—

JACQUELINE It means you both planned this weekend so that he could have his mistress down here at the same time *you* were here. Which means that—

ROBERT He's no worse than you and I.

JACQUELINE What?

ROBERT It means, if it's true—which I'm not accepting for a moment—that you've absolutely no right to be angry with him for behaving—which I'm not saying he was for a minute—just as you and I were planning to behave—which I'm not admitting for a second!

JACQUELINE No, we weren't. I was planning to go to my mother's.

ROBERT Which you cancelled the moment you knew I was coming.

JACQUELINE Which you were only doing because Bernard invited you. *I* didn't.

ROBERT We can't blame Bernard for having a lover who was pretending to be my lover so you wouldn't know she was his lover, while all the time I was your lover pretending to be her lover so that he wouldn't know you had a lover. Especially when his *real* lover was all the time pretending to be—to be...

JACQUELINE Pretending to be what?

ROBERT I've forgotten. I've lost count of how many lovers there are.

JACQUELINE Well I'll tell you this, lover. No lover's going to get the better of this lover in her own house. I'll see to that!

JACQUELINE *storms off into the kitchen.*

ROBERT *sighs and pours himself another drink.*

BERNARD *comes down the stairs in yet another clean shirt.*

BERNARD Is the coast clear?

ROBERT I don't know about the coast, but it's damned foggy round here.

BERNARD Go easy on the insects in future, will you—I'm running out of shirts.

ROBERT Bernard, I'd better warn you...

BERNARD What?

ROBERT Jacqueline's got hold of the wrong end of the stick about Suzette...

BERNARD Suzette?

ROBERT Yes. She thinks that Suzette...

SUZETTE comes out of bedroom 2. She is dressed in a dainty waitress's outfit: black skirt with white frilly blouse, white cuffs, tiny white apron and white waitress's head-piece.

The men stare.

SUZETTE What about me?

BERNARD You can't wear that! You're a guest, not the waitress.

SUZETTE I said it was the only other outfit I had.

BERNARD Hopeless! We must do something with it. *(He approaches her)* Robert, help me.

SUZETTE *(apprehensive)* What are you going to do?

BERNARD *(ripping off the apron)* That will have to go for a start.

ROBERT *(pulling off the cuffs)* And those.

BERNARD *(pulling off the head-piece, which lets her hair down)* And that. Now, let's see...

They circle her, eyeing her critically. **BERNARD** *ends up round the back.*

Yes...

SUZETTE Now what?

There is a tearing sound from the back as he separates the velcro down her blouse. She jumps.

Ooo! Here, what...?

BERNARD Quiet! Stand still!

SUZETTE Oo!

BERNARD Turn round.

He turns her so that her back is to the audience. He and
ROBERT *each take a sleeve and, in one movement, they*
pull the entire blouse off her.

SUZETTE Eek! *(She covers herself with her arms)* Look here—for
this I want—

BERNARD Don't you dare mention money again, or we'll have
the rest of it off too.

SUZETTE Ooo!

He signals to **ROBERT**, *who comes round to her back*
and takes hold of the waistband of her skirt, whilst
BERNARD *does the same at the front.*

BERNARD Right—one, two, three, heave!

Between them they pull the skirt up her body and over
her bust. **Note:** *it is one of the elasticated "tube" dresses*
that can be worn a number of ways. She is now dressed
in a very tight, black, mini-skirted dress which leaves
her arms and shoulders bare. They turn her to face the
audience. The effect is knock-out.

That's better!

ROBERT That's much better!

SUZETTE *(looking down at herself)* Here, that's quite chic, isn't
it? *(She tries an elegant walk around the room, but the skirt*
is so tight she can only manage a constricted waddle) I don't
know if I can sit down. *(She tries)* Oooo! I won't have room
for any dinner.

BERNARD God, the dinner! I'd better see how Suzanne's getting
on in there. *(He collects the waitress's accessories)* I'll take
these for her.

BERNARD *goes into the kitchen.*

ROBERT *(after him)* Bernard, I must tell you—Jacqueline thinks
Suzette is...

BERNARD *has gone.*

SUZETTE I'm what?

ROBERT Never mind—you're better off not knowing.

SUZETTE *(adopting her idea of an elegant pose; in a low, husky voice)* I could quite take to this life, you know, lover.

ROBERT Uncle.

SUZETTE Be so kind as to pour me another Cointreau.

ROBERT You've had enough of that stuff.

SUZETTE Oh, I can drink all my lovers under the table—lover.

ROBERT Uncle.

SUZETTE Oh, very well, if you insist. Such a shame, because you're really quite a dishy hunk, Unc. And since you and I are sharing the piggery tonight, it does seem a waste not to make the most of it.

She approaches ROBERT *who is standing beside the sofa.*

How do you feel about a spot of incest? *(She flings her arms round his neck)*

JACQUELINE *and* BERNARD *enter from the kitchen.*

ROBERT *steps hurriedly back.* SUZETTE *falls flat on her face across the sofa. The others stare.*

Missed.

ROBERT *(after a pause, feebly)* She's found more insects.

SUZETTE *struggles to stand up again in the tight dress.*

JACQUELINE *(staring at her dress)* That's an unusual dress. Is that a Chanel?

SUZETTE It's half a Chanel.

JACQUELINE Well, is anyone sober enough for dinner?

ROBERT Oh, thank God, yes.

SUZETTE How simply too, too divine! *(She takes* **ROBERT** *by the arm)* You can sit beside me, hunky-unky.

BERNARD *(to* **ROBERT***, smugly)* Glad to see you're getting on so well together.

> **JACQUELINE** *stamps angrily on* **BERNARD***'s foot. He hops in pain.*

What was that for?

JACQUELINE *(sweetly)* Sorry—I thought I saw another one.

> **SUZANNE** *enters from the kitchen, wearing* **SUZETTE***'s white apron, head-piece, and cuffs over her dress. She looks black as thunder, and carries a dinner-gong.*

SUZANNE Dinner is served! *(She gives a loud bang on the gong)*

Curtain.

ACT II

The same. Two hours later.

When the curtain rises the stage is empty.

The kitchen door opens and **ROBERT** *and* **SUZETTE** *come out, cheek to cheek, doing a highly-exaggerated tango. They are both very drunk. They tango across the stage, round the sofa, and back towards the kitchen, where they come face to face with an irate-looking* **JACQUELINE**. *They stop, giggling inanely.*

ROBERT Lovely dinner!

SUZETTE Simply too, too delicious!

JACQUELINE *(icily)* Do you normally dance like that with your relations?

SUZETTE Oh, Uncle Robert has all sorts of relations with his relations.

ROBERT *(to* **JACQUELINE***)* And nobody else was available, were they? *(Looking at the kitchen door)* Is that coffee I hear being served?

SUZETTE And cognac?

ROBERT After you, Niece.

SUZETTE No, after you, Uncle.

They take hold of each other again and tango off.

JACQUELINE *(furious)* Grrrr!

BERNARD enters carrying a brandy glass. He looks back after the dancers and chuckles.

BERNARD They're well away.

JACQUELINE Everyone seems to be well away, don't they?

BERNARD Yes, indeed. *(He sighs happily as he sits back on the sofa and holds out his glass)* Pour me a brandy and soda, darling.

JACQUELINE *(taking it with a sweet smile)* By all means, sweetheart. *(She goes to the drinks and pours a brandy)*

BERNARD Marvellous evening.

JACQUELINE Yes. Despite the odd set-backs with the dinner.

BERNARD Ah, yes. Don't know how the cook managed to get the cheese soufflé mixed up with the raspberry pavlova.

JACQUELINE Her version of nouvelle cuisine, she said.

BERNARD Still it all worked out in the end. Things usually do.

JACQUELINE Do they indeed? *(She brings his brandy and the soda syphon)*

BERNARD *(taking the glass)* Thank you. *(He loosens his tie)* Whew! Quite warm after all that booze.

JACQUELINE Well this should cool you down a bit. Soda?

He holds out his glass. She deliberately squirts the soda syphon straight on to his shirt front. He sits there, dripping.

Oh dear. Missed. Sorry.

BERNARD *(after a long pause)* I've run out of clean shirts. I'll go and put on my wet suit.

He gives her a worried look and goes upstairs yet again. **SUZANNE** *enters from the kitchen. She looks exhausted, her hair awry, her face smudged, her apron askew, her head-piece decidedly limp. She holds a cup of coffee in one hand.*

SUZANNE Would madam like her coffee in here?

JACQUELINE *(taking it; sweetly)* Thank you, Suzanne.

SUZANNE *turns back to the kitchen.*

Oh, Suzanne—we've had a little accident in here with the soda syphon. Would you mind mopping up the sofa for me?

SUZANNE *(too exhausted to argue)* Yes, madam. *(In a dream she uses her apron to dab at the sofa)*

JACQUELINE *paces up and down, then gives another cry of frustration.*

JACQUELINE Ooooo!

SUZANNE I beg your pardon.

JACQUELINE I'm going to have some blood before tonight's finished!

SUZANNE Wasn't the dinner enough for you, madam?

JACQUELINE It was too much! How I got through it without exploding, I'll never know.

SUZANNE What's wrong?

JACQUELINE What's wrong! I'm an utter fool, that's what's wrong!

SUZANNE Why?

JACQUELINE To sit there all evening in the same room as my husband and his mistress, and carry on trying to behave as if everything's normal... I must be mad!

SUZANNE His mistress?

JACQUELINE Yes!

SUZANNE You—you mean, you knew?

JACQUELINE Of course, I knew!

SUZANNE All along?

JACQUELINE All along.

SUZANNE How?

JACQUELINE I found proof.

SUZANNE Oh, my God...!

JACQUELINE And yet I let him sit there, being served by you, and laughing and joking and filling his face without a care in the world. What a fool I am!

SUZANNE Oh, now—don't get too upset about it, please.

JACQUELINE Don't get upset! Wouldn't you be upset?

SUZANNE Well, yes, but—

JACQUELINE Would you just ignore it?

SUZANNE No, but—

JACQUELINE Go on then—what would you do in my place?

SUZANNE I'd, er...well, it's a very difficult situation.

JACQUELINE No, it's not, it's quite simple. If you were me, and your husband brought his mistress to your own home and expected her to stay the weekend under the very same roof, what would you do?

SUZANNE Well, I suppose I'd, er...

JACQUELINE You'd poison the two of them, that's what you'd do.

SUZANNE Well, I don't know that I'd...my God, you didn't, did you?

JACQUELINE What?

SUZANNE Poison the dinner?

JACQUELINE I didn't need to. You made a pretty good job of that.

SUZANNE *(indignantly)* I did my best!

JACQUELINE Anyway, the point is, what would you do about Robert's niece?

SUZANNE Well I'd... *(Bewildered)* Where does Robert's niece come into it?

JACQUELINE Of course, you don't know, do you? She's his niece.

SUZANNE Who?

JACQUELINE Her! The preposterous, clockwork Barbie-doll in there!

SUZANNE The cook...? I mean the cookie girlfriend?

JACQUELINE She's not his girlfriend—she's his niece! He told me before dinner.

SUZANNE So what's she doing here?

JACQUELINE That's what I'm trying to tell you. She's actually my husband's mistress.

SUZANNE What?

JACQUELINE That's right.

SUZANNE That's impossible.

JACQUELINE I told you—I've got proof.

SUZANNE That he sleeps with her?

JACQUELINE Irrevocable. A love note from her to him.

SUZANNE But she's with Robert.

JACQUELINE That's just a front. Robert brought her along to disguise the fact that she's really sleeping with my husband.

SUZANNE The bastard!

JACQUELINE Who—Robert or my husband?

SUZANNE Both.

JACQUELINE Exactly.

SUZANNE But especially your husband.

JACQUELINE Exactly!

SUZANNE How could he?

JACQUELINE That's what I thought.

SUZANNE I'll kill him!

JACQUELINE So will...what do you mean, you'll kill him?

SUZANNE I mean... I'd kill him if I were you.

JACQUELINE I'm going to.

SUZANNE The rat! The pig! The swine!

JACQUELINE Well don't get carried away. He's my husband.

SUZANNE Yes, but how could he *do* this to us...to you? The nerve of the man!

JACQUELINE You've obviously been through this sort of situation yourself.

SUZANNE Yes, I... That's right, I have. That's why I sympathize with you.

JACQUELINE So what would you do in my place?

SUZANNE I... I'll tell you exactly what I'd do...

The kitchen door opens, and ROBERT *and* SUZETTE *tango out again.*

They do their turn of the room, watched by the other two, and then collapse on the sofa together, giggling and breathless.

SUZETTE Oh, I'm simply, simply exhausted!

ROBERT *(flapping his shirt-front)* And hot!

The other two look at each other and smile.

JACQUELINE Hot?

ROBERT Boiling!

JACQUELINE *(sweetly)* Well, how would you like a little something to cool you down?

ROBERT What a good idea!

JACQUELINE picks up the soda syphon and hands the ice-bucket to SUZANNE. They advance on the others from behind. SUZANNE takes an ice-cube from the ice-bucket with the tongs, leans over SUZETTE from behind and delicately drops the ice down the front of her dress.

SUZETTE Oooo! Ooooo!!

JACQUELINE squirts the soda syphon on to the top of ROBERT's head.

ROBERT Ahhhh!

SUZETTE Oooo!

They are both leaping around the room.

ROBERT *(finally)* What did we do?

JACQUELINE *(sweetly)* You said you needed cooling down. *(Grimly)* You also needed sobering up.

ROBERT I'll have to go and change.

JACQUELINE And have a cold shower while you're at it.

ROBERT goes off to bedroom 1.

SUZANNE *(to SUZETTE)* And as for you, you can go and wash up. I've done enough.

SUZETTE Here! I'm a guest!

SUZANNE *(threatening her with the ice-tongs)* You're a *what?*

SUZETTE *(hurriedly)* I'll go and wash up.

SUZETTE goes off to the kitchen.

JACQUELINE and SUZANNE collapse into giggles.

SUZANNE I feel much better for that.

JACQUELINE *(sobering)* I don't.

SUZANNE What?

JACQUELINE It's not them I'm angry with. It's my husband.

SUZANNE Oh, yes.

JACQUELINE The rat!

SUZANNE The swine!

JACQUELINE You were about to tell me what you would do in this situation.

SUZANNE So I was. I'd get my own back.

JACQUELINE How?

SUZANNE Give him a taste of his own medicine. Treat him the way he treats you.

JACQUELINE Give him gloves for Christmas?

SUZANNE No! Take a lover!

JACQUELINE A lover?

SUZANNE Yes.

JACQUELINE Ah...

SUZANNE Exactly. Let him know what it feels like.

JACQUELINE Well, between you and me...

SUZANNE Yes?

JACQUELINE I already have.

SUZANNE You have?

JACQUELINE Yes.

SUZANNE Well done!

JACQUELINE I beat him to it actually.

SUZANNE But did he know?

JACQUELINE Know?

SUZANNE When he started *his* affair?

JACQUELINE No.

SUZANNE Then that's absolutely no excuse for him!

JACQUELINE That's right!

SUZANNE So he deserves all he gets.

JACQUELINE Yes, he does!

SUZANNE And it's up to us to see that he gets it.

JACQUELINE Yes, it is! *(She frowns)* For a cook you seem to be getting very involved in all this.

SUZANNE We girls must stick together.

JACQUELINE It's very kind of you.

SUZANNE All part of the service.

> **BERNARD** *comes cautiously down the stairs, dressed in pyjamas and dressing-gown*

BERNARD *(warily)* I hope that's the last time I get soaked. I've nothing left to wear after this.

JACQUELINE Then you'd better watch your step, hadn't you, darling?

BERNARD Do I get the feeling I've done something wrong?

JACQUELINE *(innocently)* I don't know. Have you?

BERNARD I can't think what. I thought I'd behaved impeccably this evening.

JACQUELINE *(to* SUZANNE*)* So cool, isn't he?

SUZANNE So blasé.

BERNARD Eh?

JACQUELINE *(airily)* Nothing, darling, nothing. You carry on behaving impeccably whilst you can. And since you've dressed for action, I'll do the same. *(She heads for the stairs)*

BERNARD Where are you going?

JACQUELINE To slip into something more comfortable. And seductive.

BERNARD Seductive? Who for?

JACQUELINE Whoever may want to seduce me.

JACQUELINE waves a casual hand and wafts up the stairs.

BERNARD She's behaving very strangely.

SUZANNE Because as a woman she wants to be thought seductive?

BERNARD No, no—just...

SUZANNE After all, we all want that, don't we?

BERNARD *(coming close)* You don't need to worry about that, my angel... *(He gets her head-piece in his face)* Though that outfit doesn't do a lot for you.

SUZANNE You thought it was fine while I was serving dinner.

BERNARD I'm sorry about dinner.

SUZANNE How do you think I did?

BERNARD Astonishing. You gave a new meaning to the words *haute cuisine*. Did you get anything to eat yourself?

SUZANNE No.

BERNARD Why not?

SUZANNE I thought it might taste as bad as it looked.

BERNARD *(holding her close)* I'll make it all up to you tonight, my sweet. I've fixed it so I can slip between bedrooms without anyone knowing.

SUZANNE *(sweetly)* Yes, you have, haven't you? Flit happily between all the bedrooms like a little butterfly without anyone knowing what you're up to.

BERNARD That's right.

SUZANNE Except me...

BERNARD Except you.

SUZANNE And your wife.

BERNARD And my...my wife?

SUZANNE *(nodding)* She knows all about it.

BERNARD She knows?

SUZANNE Everything.

BERNARD *Everything!*

SUZANNE Yes.

BERNARD How could she possibly know?

SUZANNE She has proof.

BERNARD What proof?

SUZANNE A love letter.

BERNARD Oh my God! Didn't you deny it?

SUZANNE Deny what?

BERNARD Everything!

SUZANNE I didn't know everything. But I do now. *(She smacks him hard in the face)* Bastard!

    BERNARD *staggers back, dazed.*

BERNARD What? What did I say?

SUZANNE What a nerve! And you really thought you could get away with it.

BERNARD What are you talking about?

SUZANNE You and Robert's niece—that's what I'm talking about!

BERNARD Robert's niece?

SUZANNE Are you going to deny it?

BERNARD Deny what?

SUZANNE Sleeping with her.

BERNARD Sleep...! I didn't even know Robert had a niece.

She slaps his face again.

SUZANNE You've just given her dinner!

BERNARD Who?

SUZANNE That—that creature in there!

BERNARD The cook?

She slaps his face again.

Will you stop hitting me!

SUZANNE She's no more a cook than I am!

BERNARD Well that's not saying much.

SUZANNE *(threatening him again)* Watch it!

BERNARD Sorry, sorry. What do you mean she's not a cook?

SUZANNE Don't pretend. I'm telling you I know all about her.

BERNARD What *are* you blathering about? How the hell can
she be Robert's niece if she's the cook, and how the hell
can you know all about her if *I* didn't even know he had a
niece, which he hasn't anyway, and how the hell can I be
sleeping with his niece if I'm sleeping with you and Robert's
sleeping with his niece, which she isn't in the first place?

SUZANNE Yes.

BERNARD What do you mean, yes?

SUZANNE Yes, she is his niece, and yes, you are sleeping with
her, and yes, you're trying to sleep with me at the same time,
and yes, you're a prize shit! Your wife has told me everything.

BERNARD *(pacing)* This is insanity! I'm going out of my mind!
(He stops) Wait a minute—a love letter! You mentioned a
love letter.

SUZANNE Yes.

BERNARD From you to me?

SUZANNE No, from her to you.

BERNARD *(puzzled)* From Jacqueline to me?

SUZANNE From Robert's *niece* to you!

BERNARD Ah! But she doesn't know about you and me?

SUZANNE Robert's niece doesn't know?

BERNARD *(frantic) Jacqueline* doesn't know!

SUZANNE Oh, no—not so far as I know.

BERNARD *(with a sigh of relief)* Thank God for that at any rate!

SUZANNE However I know about *her.*

BERNARD What?

SUZANNE And in the circumstances I think you should too.

BERNARD What?

SUZANNE She has a lover also.

BERNARD Robert's niece has a lover?

SUZANNE Your *wife*, you fool!

BERNARD Jacqueline...

SUZANNE Yes.

BERNARD How do you know?

SUZANNE She just told me.

BERNARD I don't believe it.

SUZANNE Not so funny when you're on the receiving end, is it?

BERNARD Jacqueline has a lover?

SUZANNE Yes.

BERNARD My little Jacqueline?

SUZANNE *(cheerfully)* Yep.

BERNARD Who is he? I'll kill him!

The door to bedroom 1 opens and ROBERT *comes out wearing his pyjamas and dressing-gown.*

Why are you dressed for bed?

ROBERT I might ask you the same thing.

SUZANNE It seems like a very good idea. I'm exhausted. Mind if I get ready for bed too?

BERNARD *(going to her)* That's the best suggestion I've heard all evening.

SUZANNE *(slapping his face)* Don't read too much into it.

SUZANNE *goes upstairs, taking off the waitress's things.*

BERNARD *marches to the kitchen door nursing his cheek.*

BERNARD *(calling brusquely)* Suzette, come in here!

SUZETTE *comes out of the kitchen with a dish mop in her hand.*

(turning to ROBERT*)* Right—what's this about the cook being your niece?

ROBERT Suzanne is my niece?

BERNARD Not that cook—this cook.

ROBERT I thought this cook was meant to be my mistress.

BERNARD So did I, but Suzanne says she's your niece.

ROBERT I haven't got a niece.

BERNARD *I* know that!

ROBERT How did Suzanne know?

BERNARD What?

ROBERT About Suzette being my niece?

BERNARD You just said you haven't *got* a niece!

ROBERT I haven't, but Jacqueline thinks I have.

BERNARD *Jacqueline* thinks you have?

ROBERT *(caught)* Oh dear. Er...

BERNARD Why does Jacqueline think that?

ROBERT Because, er—well, because...

SUZETTE *(brightly)* Because I didn't want my husband to know Robert was supposed to be my lover.

ROBERT *(beaming)* That's it! *(A beat)* What?

They stare. She beams at them.

BERNARD You have a husband?

SUZETTE Oh yes.

ROBERT Oh, my God!

BERNARD You never mentioned him before.

SUZETTE You never asked.

BERNARD Oh, my God!

SUZETTE And as he'd probably kill Robert if he found out I was supposed to be his mistress—

ROBERT Oh, my *God!*

SUZETTE —I thought it would be best if everyone who didn't need to think he was my lover thought he was my uncle instead.

BERNARD Oh, I see! That's quite bright of you, Suzette.

ROBERT That's *very* bright of you, Suzette.

SUZETTE Thank you. That'll be another two hundred francs, please.

ROBERT looks at BERNARD. BERNARD shakes his head and gestures at ROBERT.

ROBERT *(resigned)* Well only if you promise not to let your husband kill me.

SUZETTE Oh, he hasn't killed anyone yet.

ROBERT Good. *(He gives her the money)*

SUZETTE Just broken a few bones here and there.

ROBERT Oh, my God!

BERNARD What I still don't understand is this business about me having an affair with your niece.

ROBERT Who?

BERNARD Your niece!

ROBERT I haven't got a niece.

BERNARD Oh, for God's sake...!

SUZETTE *Who* are you having an affair with?

BERNARD You.

SUZETTE *(outraged)* You're having an affair with me now!

ROBERT Good God, you don't mess about, do you?

BERNARD *(exasperated)* That's what Jacqueline thinks!

ROBERT Oh, I see.

SUZETTE Your wife thinks that?

BERNARD Yes.

SUZETTE Why?

BERNARD *(wearily)* That's what I'm trying to find out.

SUZETTE Well, please let me know when you do, because I'd like to know too. And so would my husband.

BERNARD Oh, my God!

ROBERT I think I can tell you actually.

BERNARD You can?

ROBERT Jacqueline thinks you're having an affair with Suzette because she found your note from Suzanne saying thank you for the coat which you gave Suzanne, which Jacqueline thought I gave to Suzette.

BERNARD What?

ROBERT More or less.

BERNARD Jacqueline found the note?

ROBERT Yes.

BERNARD I see! *(Pause)* No I don't.

ROBERT Why not?

BERNARD How did she know the note was to me?

ROBERT She found it in your jacket pocket.

BERNARD I see! No I don't.

ROBERT Why not?

BERNARD Why did she think the note was from Suzette?

ROBERT Because we made out the coat was Suzette's.

BERNARD I see! No I don't.

ROBERT *(exasperated)* Why *not*?

BERNARD What was she doing looking through my jacket pockets in the first place?

SUZETTE Why shouldn't she? I always look through my husband's pockets.

BERNARD *(loftily)* My wife is not like that. She trusts me.

SUZETTE Stupid woman!

ROBERT Quite. And in any case she found it when she was hanging up your jacket to dry.

SUZETTE *Thoughtful* woman.

ROBERT And an angry woman.

BERNARD I'm beginning to understand. That's why she doused me with the soda syphon.

ROBERT You too?

BERNARD What do you mean, me too?

ROBERT *(caught)* Ah. Er...

SUZETTE He means she did the same to me.

BERNARD Soda down your front?

SUZETTE Worse. Ice.

BERNARD *(shuddering)* Urrrh! Why?

SUZETTE The same reason probably. She thinks you and I are having an affair.

BERNARD Ah, I see!

SUZETTE It's not surprising she's cross.

BERNARD Wait a minute. What right has *she* to be cross?

ROBERT What?

BERNARD *I'm* the one who should be cross. In fact, I should be furious! In fact, I am!

ROBERT Why?

BERNARD She only has an insignificant little note to go on, that could mean anything. I have proof!

ROBERT Of your own affair?

BERNARD No, you fool! Of *her* affair!

ROBERT *(staring at him, stunned)* Her affair?

BERNARD Yes. I know all about it.

ROBERT You do?

BERNARD Going on right under my nose. And I can tell you I'm hopping mad!

ROBERT Oh God!

SUZETTE Oh God!

BERNARD You may well say, oh God, my friend... *(He picks up the ice-tongs and advances on* ROBERT*)* I never realized how much it would affect me. It's made me so mad that I could do unmentionable things.

ROBERT Oh lord!

SUZETTE Oh lord!

BERNARD *(grabbing* ROBERT *by the tie and pulling his face close to his)* Can you imagine what it's like? Your own wife, who you've trusted all these years! I never thought I was capable of murder, but I am now!

SUZETTE *(rushing around distracted)* Oh God!

ROBERT Now steady on, Bernard, there's no need to take it so badly...

BERNARD Oh there isn't, eh? Well put yourself in my place.

ROBERT Yes, yes, I realize that it must be very painful, but please don't get carried away.

BERNARD Carried away! I'm not the one who's going to get carried away!

SUZETTE Oh God!

ROBERT Control yourself, please...!

BERNARD *(waving the ice-tongs)* I tell you, when I find out who it is I'm going to have his private parts pickled and pinned up in a picture frame in the piggery!

ROBERT That's very nasty... *(He stops)* When you find out who it is?

BERNARD Yes.

ROBERT You mean you don't know who it is?

BERNARD Of course not. D'you think he'd still be alive if I did?

ROBERT *(relieved)* Oh, I see!

BERNARD D'you think he'd still be in one piece?

SUZETTE Oh thank God!

BERNARD What for?

SUZETTE Er...that you haven't committed a murder yet.

BERNARD I'm going to. Just as soon as I find out who he is.

ROBERT But you've still no idea who he is?

BERNARD Not yet.

ROBERT Phew!

BERNARD Is that all you've got to say?

ROBERT Er...

BERNARD You know someone's sleeping with my wife behind my back, and all you can say is phew!

ROBERT The swine.

BERNARD Exactly.

ROBERT The bastard!

BERNARD That's better.

ROBERT He deserves all he gets.

BERNARD And he's going to get it. I'm going to have his private parts pickled and—

ROBERT *(quickly)* Yes, yes—thank you, you've told us already.

JACQUELINE *comes downstairs, dressed in a very sexy négligé.*

JACQUELINE Right—I've thought it all out, and I've decided it's time to have everything out in the open.

BERNARD *(looking at her négligé)* Yes, most of it is.

JACQUELINE Let's put an end to these subterfuges. I know all about you.

BERNARD Who?

JACQUELINE *(indicating him and* **SUZETTE***)* You and her.

BERNARD What about me and her?

JACQUELINE Everything about you! She is not Robert's girlfriend, she's his niece...

SUZETTE Here we go again.

JACQUELINE And she isn't having an affair with him, she's having one with you.

SUZETTE It's like a record.

JACQUELINE *(to* **SUZETTE***)* Do you deny it?

SUZETTE I don't deny anything. I've never been so many different people and had so many different affairs with so many different men in my life! It's very nice to be so popular.

JACQUELINE *(to* **BERNARD***)* You see?

BERNARD Jacqueline, darling, I think you've got hold of the wrong end of the stick.

JACQUELINE Oh, we know who's got hold of which end of whose stick!

SUZETTE Oo, how rude!

JACQUELINE And since I know the truth about you, it's only fair that you should know the truth about me.

BERNARD What?

ROBERT Now, Jacqueline—

JACQUELINE Would you leave us please, Suzette.

SUZETTE Eh?

JACQUELINE I have some matters concerning your family which I wish to reveal, and which I think it best that you don't know about.

SUZETTE By all means. The more I get to know about what little I knew in the beginning, the less chance of my understanding what happens in the end!

SUZETTE *marches into the kitchen.*

JACQUELINE Really! I'd have credited you with a little more taste.

BERNARD She's not that bad.

JACQUELINE Ah, you admit it then!

BERNARD No, I don't! Whatever gave you such an idea?

JACQUELINE I have proof.

BERNARD Proof?

JACQUELINE "Thank you for the gorgeous, gorgeous coat, you gorgeous, gorgeous man."

BERNARD I don't know what you're talking about. *(To* **ROBERT***)* Do you know what she's talking about?

JACQUELINE Oh, he knows what I'm talking about. Only he doesn't give gorgeous, gorgeous coats to his mistresses—do you, Robert?

ROBERT Now, Jacqueline—

JACQUELINE He gives rotten pairs of gloves.

ROBERT They were jolly nice gloves!

BERNARD What have *gloves* got to do with it?

ROBERT Er...nothing.

BERNARD *(to* **JACQUELINE***)* And what did you mean just now when you said I should know the truth about you?

JACQUELINE Well, my darling—

ROBERT Now, Jacqueline—

BERNARD Quiet, you.

JACQUELINE Haven't we always said that marriage is an equal partnership?

BERNARD Yes, of course.

JACQUELINE Therefore—if you were to have a mistress, it's only fair that I should have a lover.

ROBERT Jacqueline—

BERNARD Quiet, you.

JACQUELINE Isn't it?

BERNARD Well—I suppose *if* it were true that I had a mistress...

JACQUELINE Yes?

BERNARD As a purely hypothetical situation...

JACQUELINE Of course.

BERNARD Then I suppose in that case...

JACQUELINE Well?

BERNARD It might conceivably be said that you could theoretically claim the purely academic right to have a figurative lover.

JACQUELINE Thank you.

ROBERT Jacqueline—

JACQUELINE Quiet, you! *(To* **BERNARD***)* So, since, as I said, I know all about your mythical mistress, it's only right that you should know about my illusory lover.

BERNARD You mean you *have* got a lover!

JACQUELINE *(beaming)* Yes.

BERNARD Who is he? I'll kill him!

JACQUELINE Promise?

ROBERT Please, Jacqueline.

BERNARD I'll castrate him!

JACQUELINE Jolly good.

ROBERT *(almost in tears) Please*, Jacqueline.

BERNARD Who is it?

JACQUELIN Ummm...

> *Pregnant pause.* **JACQUELINE** *keeps* **ROBERT** *in petrified suspense until her finger finally comes to rest in his direction.*

Him.

ROBERT Oh God.

BERNARD Him?

JACQUELINE Yes.

BERNARD Robert?

JACQUELINE Exactly.

BERNARD *(to* **ROBERT***)* Is this true?

ROBERT Nonsense.

BERNARD *(advancing on him with the ice-tongs)* Is it possible?

ROBERT *(backing away)* Absolutely not.

BERNARD Because if it is—

ROBERT It isn't. And even if it was, you wouldn't. And even if you did, it wouldn't be fair. You're just as bad as I am...if I was...which I'm not.

BERNARD *(waving the tongs, chasing him round the furniture)* Pickled and pinned in the piggery!

ROBERT Now, Bernard—

> *The doorbell rings loudly. They all freeze. Pause.*

BERNARD Who's that?

JACQUELINE How do I know?

BERNARD *(to* **ROBERT***)* Do you know?

ROBERT No, but I'm very glad to see them.

BERNARD I'll get it.

> **BERNARD** *goes towards the front door.* **ROBERT** *tip-toes towards the kitchen.* **BERNARD** *points the tongs.*

Stay where you are, you!

> **ROBERT** *freezes.* **BERNARD** *opens the front door.*

> **GEORGE** *stands there. He is big.*

GEORGE I've come to take her home.

BERNARD Who?

GEORGE The cook.

BERNARD Ah. Er...

GEORGE *(coming in)* Has she finished?

JACQUELINE The cook?

GEORGE Yes.

JACQUELINE I thought she was staying the night.

GEORGE Why should she do that?

JACQUELINE Well, it was so late, and—

GEORGE I always fetch her. That way she can't get into any trouble—know what I mean?

JACQUELINE Oh, yes—quite.

GEORGE Course, if she's not ready, I'm quite happy to wait... *(He looks at the scattered drinks)* as you seem to be celebrating.

JACQUELINE May we ask who you are exactly?

GEORGE I'm George.

JACQUELINE George?

GEORGE Her husband.

BERNARD ⎫
ROBERT ⎬ *(together)* Oh my God!

GEORGE *(to* **JACQUELINE***)* I work as a chef too, you see.

JACQUELINE How fascinating.

GEORGE And when I've finished, I come along to see if Suzy's finished. Is she finished?

ROBERT I think we're all finished.

GEORGE What?

JACQUELINE Yes, she's just about finished.

GEORGE Good. Are you the mistress?

JACQUELINE It depends what you mean exactly.

GEORGE Of the house?

JACQUELINE Yes, I'm the mistress of the house. And also the mistress of him. *(She indicates* **ROBERT***)* And also the wife of him. *(She indicates* **BERNARD***)*

GEORGE *(bemused)* Very cosy.

JACQUELINE *(sweetly)* Yes, isn't it?

GEORGE *(to* **BERNARD***)* I don't know how you put up with that.

BERNARD What?

GEORGE Having your wife's lover in the house.

BERNARD Neither do I.

GEORGE If it were me, I'd kill him.

BERNARD I was just about to actually.

GEORGE *(flexing his muscles)* Do you want any help?

BERNARD Thank you. I'll let you know if I do.

GEORGE Right.

ROBERT Oh God!

GEORGE *(to* JACQUELINE*)* Well if she's finished, where is she?

JACQUELINE I'm not sure. Where is she, Bernard?

BERNARD Er—who?

JACQUELINE Suzy of course!

BERNARD I, er...she's gone.

JACQUELINE Gone?

BERNARD Left.

JACQUELINE Why?

BERNARD Well, she'd er...finished. So she left. *(To* ROBERT*)* Right? Left.

ROBERT *(nodding furiously)* Left. Right. Left.

GEORGE She wouldn't have left.

BERNARD Why not?

GEORGE She knew I was coming.

BERNARD Perhaps that's why she left.

GEORGE *(dangerously)* I beg your pardon?

BERNARD *(hastily)* I meant, perhaps she left to meet you on the way.

GEORGE She never leaves when I'm coming. She must be here.

JACQUELINE Perhaps she's upstairs.

GEORGE *(suspiciously)* Upstairs?

JACQUELINE *(calling up the stairs)* Suzy!

GEORGE *(to the men)* What would she be doing upstairs?

BERNARD Can't imagine.

ROBERT Haven't the foggiest.

SUZANNE *comes down the stairs, also wearing a sexy négligé.*

JACQUELINE Yes, here she is... *(To* BERNARD*)* Why did you say she'd left?

BERNARD Er... I meant left to go upstairs.

JACQUELINE And she's changed.

BERNARD In order to change.

JACQUELINE *(to* SUZANNE*)* Well—there was no need.

SUZANNE There wasn't?

JACQUELINE Look who's here. *(She indicates* GEORGE*)*

SUZANNE *(staring)* Who?

JACQUELINE George. He's come to take you home.

Pause.

SUZANNE Take me home?

JACQUELINE Yes.

SUZANNE What for?

JACQUELINE *(puzzled)* Well...

GEORGE Who's this?

JACQUELINE Who does it look like?

GEORGE Don't ask me.

JACQUELINE It's your wife.

GEORGE My wife?

JACQUELINE Your wife, the cook.

GEORGE She's certainly not my wife. And she doesn't look much like a cook.

ROBERT Oh God!

GEORGE I certainly wouldn't let my wife do the cooking dressed like that!

SUZANNE Are you objecting?

GEORGE Not at all—very nice.

SUZANNE Thank you.

GEORGE If you like your beef rare. But are *you* the cook?

SUZANNE On and off.

GEORGE Then where's Suzy?

JACQUELINE This *is* Suzy.

GEORGE Not my Suzy.

JACQUELINE *(puzzled)* Really?

BERNARD *(hastily)* Perhaps you've come to the wrong house.

GEORGE I came to the right house to drop her off. Are you telling me I can't tell one house from another now it's time to pick her up?

BERNARD No, no.

GEORGE So where is she?

BERNARD She's not here.

ROBERT Definitely not here.

JACQUELINE It's true there is another Suzy here—

GEORGE Aha!

JACQUELINE But she can't be your Suzy.

GEORGE Why not?

JACQUELINE Firstly, she's not a cook, she's an actress.

BERNARD That's right.

JACQUELINE Secondly, she's this gentleman's niece.

ROBERT That's right.

JACQUELINE And thirdly, she's my husband's mistress.

BERNARD That's r—Oh God!

GEORGE *Very* cosy! Quite a ménage you have here.

JACQUELINE Yes, isn't it?

SUZANNE Yes, isn't it?

GEORGE Well, that certainly can't be my Suzy.

BERNARD It can't?

GEORGE Oh no. My Suzy is definitely a cook, not an actress. I know all her uncles. And if she was anybody's mistress I'd have killed them both long ago.

ROBERT Oh golly!

BERNARD What?

ROBERT I've run out of ways of saying oh God.

GEORGE Funny though.

BERNARD What?

GEORGE That you should have two Suzys here.

SUZANNE *(to* **BERNARD***)* Yes—explain that one.

BERNARD Oh, it's a very common name, Suzy.

GEORGE Is it?

ROBERT We know hundreds of Suzys.

GEORGE You do?

BERNARD Especially round here.

GEORGE Round here?

BERNARD They breed Suzys like flies round here.

GEORGE *(demonstrating)* My Suzy is about this high, and about this wide, with a long black skirt and a high white blouse.

BERNARD Ah no—our Suzy is taller than that, I think...

ROBERT And considerably thinner...

BERNARD With a very short skirt...

ROBERT And a very low top.

GEORGE No, that can't be my Suzy. If she dressed like that I'd kill her.

BERNARD
ROBERT } *(together)* It's definitely not your Suzy!

Together, they manhandle him towards the front door.

BERNARD I should try the other houses.

ROBERT There are lots round here like this.

BERNARD Dinner parties going on all over the place.

ROBERT People gorging themselves in all directions.

GEORGE Right.

They get him to the front door, and open it.

SUZETTE *comes out of the kitchen.*

SUZETTE Well, that's finished that lot. Anything else?

The three men freeze in the doorway.

GEORGE *(turning)* Suzy!

SUZETTE Georgie!

ROBERT
BERNARD } *(together)* Oh God!

GEORGE *and* **SUZY** *rush into each others arms.*

GEORGE I knew you were here!

SUZETTE Of course I'm here, flower!

GEORGE I knew you wouldn't have gone.

SUZETTE Gone where?

GEORGE These people seemed to think... They told me that...
Hold on a minute. *(He glowers round the room)*

ROBERT *(to* BERNARD*)* Here we go.

GEORGE First of all they said you'd left...

SUZETTE No, I'm still here.

GEORGE Then they said you were upstairs...

SUZETTE No, I was in there.

GEORGE Then they said you were in another house doing
another dinner...

SUZETTE No, this house.

GEORGE *(to* BERNARD*)* So what was all that nonsense in aid of?

BERNARD Well, you see, er...

GEORGE *(to* ROBERT*)* Eh?

ROBERT Well, you see, er...

GEORGE And what is more...

SUZETTE What?

GEORGE *(indicating* JACQUELINE*)* She told me you were an
actress...

SUZETTE Course not, I'm a cook.

GEORGE She also told me you were this man's niece...

SUZETTE Don't be silly, flower.

GEORGE She also told me you were *this* man's mistress!

SUZETTE How ridiculous!

GEORGE Is it?

SUZETTE Of course it is.

GEORGE Then what are you dressed like that for?

SUZETTE Ah. Well, it's a long story...

GEORGE *(increasingly angry)* And what are they all dressed like that for?

BERNARD Well, you see, old chap—

GEORGE Don't you old chap me! I *knew* there was something funny about you lot. Upstairs and downstairs, with mistresses and lovers all over the blooming place! *(Roaring)* There's a ruddy orgy going on here, isn't there?

BERNARD No, no...

GEORGE With my Suzy in the middle of it!

ROBERT *(hiding behind* **BERNARD***)* You don't understand...

GEORGE I understand all right! *(With rage)* Ahhhh!

> *He takes a wild swing at* **BERNARD***, who ducks.* **ROBERT** *catches it instead, and goes head over heels over the sofa.* **BERNARD** *gets the next one and goes over the chair. The three women all hang screaming on to* **GEORGE***. He finally goes down under a mass of female legs, arms and flying négligés.*

(muffled under the pile of bodies) All right, all right—I give in.

SUZETTE *(on top of the heap)* If we let you up, will you behave yourself, flower?

GEORGE Yes, yes.

SUZETTE Promise?

GEORGE I promise.

> *Everyone disentangles themselves, and gets up.* **ROBERT***'s head appears from behind the sofa,* **BERNARD***'s from behind the chair.*

ROBERT *(dazed)* What happened?

BERNARD Where am I?

SUZETTE *(bossing a dazed* **GEORGE** *into a chair)* I've told you before, flower—you mustn't lose your temper like that.

GEORGE Sorry, petal.

SUZETTE Don't jump to conclusions till you've found out the facts.

GEORGE Right. So what are the facts?

JACQUELINE Yes, what are the facts?

SUZETTE It's all a game.

GEORGE A game?

SUZETTE Yes! A game these people like to play after dinner. It's called Happy Families. *(To* **BERNARD***)* Isn't that so, sir?

BERNARD Er...yes, yes.

GEORGE Happy Families?

SUZETTE You see, everybody has to pretend to be related to somebody in the house, whilst at the same time having a secret affair with somebody else. And then everyone has to guess who everyone else is related to, and who they're having an affair with, and the more relatives and lovers everybody has then the more points they get.

GEORGE What happens to the winner?

SUZETTE They get let off the washing up.

GEORGE Ah.

SUZETTE It's great fun! We must play it sometime.

GEORGE So that's it?

BERNARD Yes, yes.

GEORGE It's a game?

ROBERT That's right.

GEORGE *(indicating* **BERNARD***)* He's not really your lover?

SUZETTE How could he be? I've only just met him.

GEORGE *(indicating* **ROBERT***)* And he's not really your uncle?

SUZETTE No!

JACQUELINE No?

SUZETTE *(hesitating with a look from* **JACQUELINE** *to* **ROBERT***)* Ah. Well, er...

JACQUELINE I thought he *was* your uncle. *(To* **ROBERT***)* That's why you brought her here in the first place.

ROBERT Well, you see, er...

JACQUELINE *(menacingly)* If you aren't her uncle, what *are* you?

ROBERT I'm, er...

SUZETTE Course he's my uncle!

ROBERT Course I'm her uncle.

JACQUELINE He is?

SUZETTE But sort of once removed.

GEORGE He is?

SUZETTE You haven't got your glasses on, flower. He's my favourite uncle. Uncle Robert.

GEORGE Uncle Robert?

SUZETTE You remember. The uncle that gives me those nice big tips—I mean presents whenever I go to cook for him.

GEORGE Tips?

SUZETTE *(winking)* Presents.

GEORGE *(cottoning on)* Oh, yes! That uncle!

SUZETTE That's right. The generous uncle.

GEORGE *(going to* **ROBERT***)* Of course, the generous uncle!

ROBERT The very generous uncle. *(He puts more notes into* **GEORGE***'s top pocket)*

GEORGE *(kissing him loudly on both cheeks)* Yes, I recognize you up close. Suzy's favourite uncle. *(He claps him heartily* *on the shoulders)* Haven't seen you for years! How are you? *(He claps him again)*

ROBERT *(shaken)* Just about surviving.

GEORGE Well that's good.

ROBERT Very good.

GEORGE Silly of me.

ROBERT Don't mention it.

> **GEORGE** *gives him a last thunderous clap, and turns back to* **SUZETTE.**

GEORGE *(hugging her)* My little Suzy!

SUZETTE You big dope!

BERNARD *(to* **ROBERT***)* Thank God for that!

GEORGE *(to* **JACQUELINE***)* Well then—if you've finished with her services...

JACQUELINE It looks as if we have.

GEORGE Then I'll take her home. All right, Suzy?

SUZETTE *(to* **BERNARD** *and* **ROBERT***)* Do you need me for anybody... I mean anything else tonight?

BERNARD No thank you, Suzy—that's all. You've been a great help. Hasn't she, Robert?

ROBERT A life saver.

SUZETTE Right then. We can go, flower. I'll just get my things.

> **SUZETTE** *goes into bedroom 2.*

GEORGE You all look as if you're ready for bed anyway.

JACQUELINE Yes, we are. We just haven't decided yet who's going to bed with who.

GEORGE Ha, ha! It sounds a good game, this.

JACQUELINE A wonderful game.

SUZETTE *returns from the bedroom with her bag and the coat over her shoulders.*

SUZETTE Good-night then.

BERNARD Good-n— *(He sees the coat and freezes)*

SUZETTE Thank you for a wonderful evening. And for my lovely coat.

BERNARD *(weakly)* Don't mention it.

SUZETTE Just send my wage to the agency. Service is included.

With a wave of the hand, SUZETTE *and* GEORGE *are gone.*

BERNARD *smiles weakly at* SUZANNE.

SUZANNE That's wonderful! Thanks a lot!

JACQUELINE What?

BERNARD Er...she meant it's wonderful they've gone.

SUZANNE And thanks a lot to them both.

JACQUELINE Oh.

BERNARD Now where were we? Oh, yes. *(He picks up the tongs and advances on* ROBERT*)* You and my wife!

ROBERT Now, now—Bernard...

JACQUELINE *comes between them with peals of forced laughter.*

JACQUELINE Ha, ha—you didn't believe that, did you?

BERNARD What?

ROBERT You didn't think she was serious?

BERNARD You weren't serious?

JACQUELINE Of course not.

ROBERT Of course not.

BERNARD You were joking?

ROBERT Of course she was!

JACQUELINE Of course I was!

BERNARD Ah. *(Relaxing)* Ha, ha. I thought you must be. Old Robert would never do a thing like that.

ROBERT Course I wouldn't.

JACQUELINE Course he wouldn't. I was just trying to get my own back.

BERNARD I see... What for?

JACQUELINE You and Robert's niece.

BERNARD Oh, yes. *(To* ROBERT*)* What *was* all that about her being your niece?

ROBERT Ah.

JACQUELINE What?

ROBERT Well, er...

JACQUELINE You mean after all that she *wasn't* your niece?

ROBERT Er...no.

JACQUELINE Nor your mistress?

ROBERT No.

JACQUELINE She was just the cook?

ROBERT Yes. Just the cook.

　　　JACQUELINE *looks at* SUZANNE.

JACQUELINE Then who's this?

　　　Pause.

BERNARD *(looking at* ROBERT*)* Er...

ROBERT *(looking at* SUZANNE*)* Er...

SUZANNE *(looking anywhere)* Er...

BERNARD His mistress.

JACQUELINE His mistress?

SUZANNE Yes.

JACQUELINE *(to* **ROBERT***)* Yes?

ROBERT Yes.

JACQUELINE So you *have* got a mistress?

ROBERT Sort of.

JACQUELINE Sort of?

ROBERT I've only got her on trial.

JACQUELINE And why have you brought your mistress here?

ROBERT Well, er...

BERNARD Why shouldn't he bring her here?

JACQUELINE *(caught)* Ah.

BERNARD Eh?

JACQUELINE Well, er...

BERNARD Is there any reason why old Robert shouldn't bring his mistress here?

JACQUELINE No, I suppose not.

BERNARD Then that's all right then.

JACQUELINE Yes, I suppose so.

BERNARD Good.

JACQUELINE But what I still don't understand is—

BERNARD What?

JACQUELINE If she's his mistress...

BERNARD Yes?

JACQUELINE Why all the pretence about the *cook* being his mistress?

BERNARD The cook?

JACQUELINE And for that matter, his niece?

BERNARD Ah.

Pregnant pause. BERNARD *look helplessly at* ROBERT.

Robert?

ROBERT Well, er... it's like this. *(He takes a deep breath and jumps in at the deep end)* You see, I didn't know you had a cook coming, so when Suzette came I jumped to the conclusion she must be Bernard's mistress who had showed up since you were supposed to be staying at your mother's, and since I knew you *weren't* at your mother's I suggested to Suzette that she should pose as *my* mistress instead so that you wouldn't suspect she was Bernard's mistress, and Suzette jumped to the conclusion *you* were my mistress and that I was suggesting *she* should pose as my mistress so that *Bernard* wouldn't suspect, and then when Suzanne showed up who *was* my mistress I said that Suzette was really Bernard's mistress so that *Suzanne* wouldn't suspect, and that since Suzette was posing as my mistress in order that you wouldn't suspect, then Suzanne would have to pose as the cook so that you *still* wouldn't suspect, but subsequently Suzette disclosed that she had an outsized husband who *also* mustn't suspect, so I assumed it singularly unwise for Suzette to be my mistress however many people suspected, so for a small consideration Suzette consented to be my niece instead so *nobody* should suspect.

Long pause.

BERNARD *(thoughtfully)* Yes, that seems very clear.

JACQUELINE *(even more thoughtfully)* Yes, I understand.

ROBERT You do?

JACQUELINE Yes.

ROBERT I'm so glad.

BERNARD So everybody's happy now?

ROBERT *(looking at* SUZANNE*)* I'm happy.

SUZANNE *(looking at* ROBERT*)* I'm very happy.

BERNARD *(to* JACQUELINE*)* Are you happy, my sweet?

JACQUELINE I suppose so...

BERNARD Good.

JACQUELINE *(puzzling)* Except for one little thing.

BERNARD What *now!*

JACQUELINE Why did you give the cook a Chanel coat as a present?

Pause.

BERNARD Me?

JACQUELINE You.

BERNARD The cook?

JACQUELINE Yes.

BERNARD What makes you think I did that?

JACQUELINE *(producing the two bits of paper)* These bits of paper I found in your jacket pocket. One is the receipt for the coat. And the other is her thank-you note, which says, "Thank you for the gorgeous, gorgeous coat, you gorgeous, gorgeous man. Suzy."

BERNARD You found those?

JACQUELINE In your pocket.

BERNARD *(stumped)* Er...yes...well... *(Hissing at* ROBERT*)* Help!

ROBERT Actually—those are mine.

JACQUELINE Yours?

ROBERT Yes.

JACQUELINE Why were *you* giving a coat to the cook?

ROBERT I wasn't. I was giving it to Suzanne.

JACQUELINE Suzanne?

SUZANNE Yes.

JACQUELINE But you said it was the cook's.

ROBERT I said that so that you wouldn't know it was Suzanne's, who was supposed to *be* the cook.

JACQUELINE I see. *(Pause)* No, I don't.

ROBERT Why not?

JACQUELINE The cook's gone off wearing it.

ROBERT I said the cook could have it as a reward for pretending to be my mistress and my niece. I'll get Suzanne another one.

SUZANNE *(beaming)* Oh, thank you.

ROBERT *(casually)* It's nothing. *(He freezes as he realizes what he's said)*

JACQUELINE I see. No, I don't.

ROBERT Why *not*?

JACQUELINE It still doesn't explain what the papers were doing in Bernard's pocket.

ROBERT Well, you see—I was afraid of my mistress finding them, so I gave them to Bernard for safe-keeping.

JACQUELINE I see. No, I don't.

ROBERT Why *not*?

JACQUELINE Suzanne *is* your mistress. Why were you afraid of her finding them?

BERNARD Yes...

SUZANNE Yes...

ROBERT *(looking meaningfully at* **JACQUELINE***)* I meant my other mistress.

Pause.

JACQUELINE Ah. I see.

BERNARD Your other mistress?

ROBERT Yes.

BERNARD Oh, you mean the cook! When *she* was being your mistress.

ROBERT Yes, quite. The cook.

BERNARD Yes, that makes sense... *(He frowns)* I think.

SUZANNE Yes. *(Frowning)* Does it?

ROBERT *(to* **JACQUELINE***)* Doesn't it?

JACQUELINE Yes, yes—that makes a lot of sense.

ROBERT Good. Then that's settled. Anything else?

Everyone looks at everyone else.

BERNARD That seems to be it.

JACQUELINE I think it is.

BERNARD I can't think of anything.

ROBERT Thank God for that!

BERNARD I think it's time we all went to bed. I'm shattered.

JACQUELINE Me too.

ROBERT Me too. *(He kisses* **JACQUELINE***'s hand)* Thank you for a wonderful evening. I'm so glad I came.

JACQUELINE Are you?

ROBERT And I'm so glad we've all kept our friendship through the excitement. It's very important, don't you think, to keep one's friendships?

JACQUELINE Yes, indeed.

BERNARD Yes, indeed.

ROBERT *(going to bedroom 1)* Good-night then. *(Passing* **SUZANNE***)* Good-night.

SUZANNE Good-night.

JACQUELINE Isn't Suzanne going with you?

ROBERT *(stopping)* Er... I'm a very restless sleeper, remember?

JACQUELINE You are...you are?

ROBERT Suzanne prefers to sleep separately.

SUZANNE I do? I do. *(Going to bedroom 2)* Good-night then.

BERNARD ⎫
JACQUELINE ⎭ *(together)* Good-night.

> **ROBERT** *and* **SUZANNE** *disappear into their respective rooms.*

BERNARD *(clearing the glasses)* Dear old Robert.

JACQUELINE *(switching off the lights)* Yes, dear old Robert.

BERNARD You know I got a funny feeling this evening that you quite fancied him.

JACQUELINE Robert? Good lord no, he's not my type.

BERNARD Ah.

JACQUELINE I got a suspicion that you quite fancied her.

BERNARD Suzanne? Not my type at all.

JACQUELINE Ah. You know, I don't think it was a good idea to ask them for the weekend, sweetheart.

BERNARD You don't?

JACQUELINE These single people lead such unsettled lives. It's very disturbing for us happily married ones.

BERNARD Yes it is, I suppose.

JACQUELINE We should let them do their cavorting elsewhere.

BERNARD Quite. We've got all we need.

JACQUELINE We don't want to spoil it.

BERNARD Let's go to bed.

JACQUELINE Yes, let's.

> **JACQUELINE** *and* **BERNARD** *kiss and go upstairs, turning off the last lights.*
>
> *The room is in semi-darkness. Pause.*
>
> *The door to bedroom 1 opens and* **ROBERT***'s head sticks out.*
>
> *He looks about, sees no-one, peers up the stairs, then goes to the door of bedroom 2. He hesitates, goes to knock, hesitates again, goes to knock again. At that moment the handle turns and he flattens himself against the wall.*
>
> **SUZANNE***'s head sticks out.*
>
> *She sees no-one and goes to the door of bedroom 1. She hesitates, goes to knock, hesitates again, then knocks.*

ROBERT Yes?

SUZANNE *(jumping)* Oo! *(Foolishly)* Oh, there you are.

ROBERT I was just, er...

SUZANNE So was I.

ROBERT What?

SUZANNE Er...wondering what's supposed to happen now.

ROBERT I'm not sure. *(Pointing upstairs)* Were you expecting...?

SUZANNE Well, I hardly think so. In the circumstances.

ROBERT No.

SUZANNE Not that I really want it. In the circumstances.

ROBERT Quite.

SUZANNE In fact, it was a pretty silly idea altogether.

ROBERT In the circumstances.

SUZANNE Did I get the impression that...?

ROBERT What?

SUZANNE Your circumstances were a bit like my circumstances.

ROBERT Sort of.

SUZANNE Ah.

ROBERT Pretty silly all round really.

SUZANNE Yes.

ROBERT We single people ought to leave those staid married people alone.

SUZANNE Yes.

ROBERT Much better doing our own thing.

SUZANNE In our own way.

ROBERT With our own sort.

Pause.

SUZANNE Well, er...

ROBERT Are you quite happy in the piggery?

SUZANNE What's it like in the cow-shed?

ROBERT Oh, it's very nice in the cow-shed.

SUZANNE I think I'd prefer it in the cow-shed.

ROBERT Oh, right. *(He moves to bedroom 2)* I'll move into the piggery.

SUZANNE No!

He stops.

I couldn't turn you out into the piggery.

ROBERT Oh...well, do you mind sharing the cow-shed?

SUZANNE I'd love to share the cow-shed. I've wanted to share the cow-shed ever since you pinched my taxi.

ROBERT So've I.

She takes his arm and they go towards bedroom 1. He stops at the door.

But I must warn you I am a very restless sleeper.

SUZANNE Who says you're going to get any sleep? *(She beams)* After all, you must have a reward.

ROBERT What for?

SUZANNE Buying me another gorgeous, gorgeous coat.

ROBERT *(his face falling)* Oh my God!

She pulls him inside.

As the lights dim there is a deafening cacophony of farmyard animals and—.

—the curtain falls.

FURNITURE AND PROPERTY LIST

ACT I

On stage: Drinks bar. *On it*: glasses, bottles of vodka, brandy,
Cointreau and tonic water, soda syphon, dish of
lemon slices
Sofa
Easy chairs
Mirror
Telephone

Off stage: Ice-bucket and tongs (**Bernard**)
Suitcase (**Bernard**)
Suitcase (**Robert**)
Shopping bag and list (**Jacqueline**)
Big shopping bag (**Suzette**)
Bags of shopping (**Bernard**)
Small suitcase (**Suzanne**)
Bowl of sauce and wooden spoon (**Suzanne**)
Dinner gong (**Suzanne**)

Personal: **Bernard:** wrist-watch, car keys, wallet containing
banknotes
Robert: wallet containing banknotes
Suzanne: wrist-watch

ACT II

Set: Fresh ice cubes in ice-bucket

Off stage: Brandy glass (**Bernard**)
Cup of coffee (**Suzanne**)
Dish-mop (**Suzette**)
Big shopping bag (**Suzette**)

Personal: **Robert:** banknotes in wallet
Jacqueline: two bits of paper

LIGHTING PLOT

Practical fittings required: lamps

Interior. The same scene throughout

ACT I

To open: Practicals on with covering spots

No cues

ACT II

To open: Practicals on with covering spots

Cue 1	**Jacqueline** switches off the lights	(Page 115)
	Snap off practicals and covering spots in sequence	
Cue 2	**Jacqueline** and **Bernard** go upstairs turning off the last lights	(Page 116)
	Snap to semi-darkness	
Cue 3	**Suzanne** pulls **Robert** inside	(Page 118)
	Fade to Black-out	

EFFECTS PLOT

ACT I

THIS
IS
NOT
THE
END